Praise for SHOULD WE FIRE GOD?

"As one who has at times doubted God, I found the honesty and thoroughness of this book refreshing. Jim Pace tackles the ever-troubling problem of pain with insight, wisdom, and humility, and without conveniently avoiding tough questions. This book will no doubt ease the minds of both believers plagued by doubts and the unconvinced whose doubts have rendered faith impossible."

—Matt Rogers, author of *When Answers Aren't Enough: Experiencing God as Good When Life Isn't*

"Questions and stories—these are some of the honest ways we humans grapple with God and faith. By this count, Jim Pace is a very honest writer, a storyteller with the courage to help us face our deepest questions."

—Winn Collier, author of *Restless Faith, Let God,* and *Holy Curiosity*

"In such a time as ours we face a great dilemma. On the one hand it seems we and the world need God all the more, and on the other, that the God we need might not be up to the task. Jim Pace provides a thoughtful and honest look at the tension so many people I know (including myself) often face. Steeped in Jim's own story of doubt, disbelief, and tragedy, this book is a refreshing look at this apparent impasse."

—Chris Backert, director and organizational architect of The Ecclesia Network

"Using painful firsthand experiences, Jim tells gripping stories and asks courageous questions while checking common clichés at the door. Asking good questions of God is better than learning good information about Him. But Jim presents the reader with both. This book made me want to pull up a chair and have a conversation with the author—and with God Himself."

—J. R. Briggs, author of *When God Says Jump* and coauthor of *The Message // REMIX: Solo*

"This book affected me deeply. It's one of the greatest treatises I've ever read on life's deepest questions about God and the whys in life. I think the Lord has produced a classic through Jim Pace. It should be read and studied by skeptics and seminarians, peasants and presidents. Very few have written so well what so many have wondered about when it comes to God and suffering."

—Jimmie Davidson, pastor of Highlands Fellowship, Abingdon, Virginia

"This book oozes honesty about the doubts and anger we often feel when injustice occurs. The book not only made me laugh and brought me to tears, more important, it caused me to think. SHOULD WE FIRE GOD? will appeal to people wherever they are on their spiritual journeys."

—Amy L. Swoope, cohost of *Freedom Today*

"In 1957, Paul Tillich's *Dynamics of Faith* made the case to a post–World War II generation that doubt was a critical component of every authentic expression of faith. Fifty years later, Jim Pace makes the same kind of case in the context of the shootings at Virginia Tech. Like Jim, this book is unflinchingly courageous in asking hard questions, compassionately pastoral in tone, and achingly honest in revealing his 'skin in the game.' What a marvelous book!"

—John P. Chandler, author of *Courageous Church Leadership: Conversations with Effective Practitioners*

"Like an accomplished novelist, Jim Pace holds your attention; like a thoughtful pastor, he deals with reality compassionately; and like a wise guide, he helps us live more honestly. If you have ever wrestled with the problem of evil, this is a must-read!"

—JR Woodward, cofounder of Kairos Los Angeles

Should We Fire God?

Finding Hope in God
When We Don't Understand

J I M P A C E

New York Boston Nashville

FaithWords
Hachette Book Group
237 Park Avenue
New York, NY 10017

www.faithwords.com.
Printed in the United States of America

First Edition: April 2010
10 9 8 7 6 5 4 3 2 1

FaithWords is a division of Hachette Book Group, Inc.
The FaithWords name and logo are trademarks of Hachette Book Group, Inc.

Library of Congress Cataloging-in-Publication Data
Pace, Jim
Should we fire God? : finding hope in God when we don't understand / Jim Pace.—1st ed.
p. cm.
Summary: "Pastor and Virginia Tech alumnus Jim Pace explains why God sometimes allows life to go terribly wrong and how to maintain faith in spite of calamity"—Provided by the publisher
ISBN 978-0-446-54614-0
1. Providence and government of God—Christianity.
2. Suffering—Religious aspects—Christianity. 3. Hope—Religious aspects—Christianity. I. Title.
BT135.P33 2010
231'.8—dc22
2009027120

I cannot thank my family enough. Tracy, Noah, Seth, and Emma: you let me write late into the night when I needed to and dealt with my crabbiness the next day. I could never, nor would I ever, dream of a better family than you.

Matt, Mike, and Chris, you are more than just copastors, you are also great friends. Your support and your wise counsel have been critical for me. I am truly fortunate to work with men like you who are so willing and able to watch over my life.

Contents

     A Note from the Author   *249*
     Notes   *251*
     About the Author   *254*

Acknowledgments

THIS WHOLE THING GOT STARTED by this wonderful woman named Michelle Rapkin, who was intrigued enough by some things she heard me say on CNN to send me an e-mail. Michelle, thank you.

I have also been wonderfully and wisely guided through this process by Chris Park. You have been an agent, an editor, and, at a couple of key points, a great voice of truth.

Holly Halverson took something that had some good bones and hints of more and deftly helped that possibility become reality.

Sarah Holloway—I still am not sure where a semicolon should be used and where not, but I am glad you do. You were an enormous help to me in cleaning the book up and helping to shape its flow. You made it better. Thank you.

Foreword

WE LIVE IN A BROKEN WORLD. Because of that, we've all been brought to our knees by tragedies. What do you do when you're struggling with overwhelming circumstances and emotions? How should you respond when your faith is tested and God seems absent or in no hurry to act?

In this book, Jim Pace offers helpful insights on the age-old question of God's role in human pain. Jim shares from his own personal battle in understanding God's faithfulness in the midst of pain, as well as dealing with the issues raised after the tragic shooting at his alma mater, Virginia Tech. Many of his congregation attended there during the shooting.

Jim shows how the Bible answers these kinds of situations. The answers are clear, he says, but they are often not what we expect or desire.

The fact is, no one is immune to pain or insulated from suffering. But God is there to provide real comfort and hope no matter what we face in this life. He uses even tragedy for our growth and His glory, when we give Him all the pieces. While God may *seem* absent, He is never really gone. While He sometimes *seems* silent, He is always speaking His love for us. While He sometimes fails to do what we think He should, He is always actively engaged in our problems, wanting to draw us closer to Him. In pain, we learn things about God that we will not learn any other way.

Rick Warren
Saddleback Church
The Purpose Driven Life

Introduction

Maybe our world is violently spinning out of control and those of us with faith in God are just the last ones to get the memo. Maybe there really is no one in charge. Maybe we are like kids in the back of a car careening down the highway with no one at the wheel, frustrated at all the swerving but confidently telling ourselves that someone *must really* be up there. How could there not be? Maybe April 16, 2007, is and should be the final nail in a coffin full of them already: the final example of a God who either doesn't exist or is so impotent at his job, he's hardly worth following.

God and I go back and forth about a lot of things. I am both awed by his power that so often surprises me, and frustrated when that power isn't used the way I think it should be. I look at the world around me and very often wish God would step into the game in a more noticeable way.

And I am sure I am not the only one.

The really sticky issues for me have always dealt with why a God who claims to be capable, loving, and aware could allow such suffering to occur for so long. Why God seems to make it so difficult to connect with him at times, to hear his voice when I feel justified and am asking for that. Why he would do things like place a gigantic tempter of a tree in the direct proximity of Adam and Eve and expect them to just leave it alone. And above all else, where in the world is he when things go horribly wrong?

When I look at my life and the job I have been entrusted to do, I know that if I were as seemingly unconcerned with what *I* am responsible for, I would have a problem. Were I to approach *my* job the way it sometimes seems God approaches his; if I were as tough to get in touch with, as tough to predict—well, at some point I would be doing some serious job hunting.

In light of everything going on in our world today, the question begs to be asked: should God be fired?

There are times when I think I would use God's power differently if I were in his metaphorical shoes. That issue made it tough for me to start a relationship with God through Jesus. I felt, *If I disagree with how he is handling the planet, do I really want to spend time pursuing him?* I also had a really hard time when I saw Christians. I almost never saw anyone demonstrate a life I would want. I usually saw a bunch of angry male chauvinists who always seemed to be against things that I was for.

If they weren't yelling, they seemed to be asking for my money. Some college friends and I even made up a drinking game: we would watch televangelists and have a drink every time they asked for a donation. That led to quite a few hangovers! Neither type of Christian really made me want to follow their example.

But eventually I was drawn in by the teachings of Jesus. I felt he had something new to teach me. He is the reason I have tried to come to terms (to the extent I have) with these tough issues. I want to know and understand Jesus more.

You may be like many of my friends who are educated, informed about what is happening around the globe, and spiritually intrigued. And like many of my friends, you might feel that a connection with the God of the Bible isn't the most useful way to spend your time. If that sounds at all like you, I think this book could help.

Others of you are like me: followers of Jesus who still have issues with God. You are also informed and frustrated with the amount of suffering that God hasn't alleviated, even though you are grateful for the good he has done. And if you are like me, you might also have some issues muddying the water a bit. Concepts as profound and defining as these—undeserved suffering and loss—often bring up other less-important issues such as a general mistrust of people, cynicism, and doubt, which can add confusion to a process that already has plenty of its own. For you, I hope to shape some of the discussion in a new way.

Difficult questions about God's job performance come at us in the midst of lives that are raging at full speed, and I believe God would honestly like to interact with us about them. No spinning...but no easy answers either. In our age of Google and "Ask" algorithms, we get used to finding out things quickly. Unfortunately Wikipedia cannot help us much with this one. Nope, this one requires that we take some time, maybe slow down a bit, and try to carefully sort all this out.

The best I can hope and pray for in this book is that we can talk over these ancient questions freshly. I will attempt to bring some new insight to bear on what you or someone you are close to is struggling with. Then the best thing I can do is have the wisdom and restraint to just get out of the way and let you and the transcendent God of the universe take it from there. I think there are real answers to much of what we wonder. Maybe not the answers we would like—neat, clean, and nicely packaged—but meaningful answers nonetheless. I promise: no hard sells in this book. Just some helpful dialogue.

Before we go any further, let me give you a sense of who I am. That way you can be picturing my bald head as I take you through some of the worst days of my life. The truth is, if you picture Scott Van Pelt from SportsCenter on ESPN and pop some earrings on him, you basically have me.

I drive a '92 Mazda Protégé. By "drive," I mean it has been sitting beside our house for the past couple of months waiting for me to find time to get it fixed. So now I guess I drive a red ten-speed. My three kids, Noah, Seth, and Emma, are amazing. Watch for Noah in the movies someday, Seth will be on ESPN, and Emma will have an art exhibit coming to a gallery near you. My wife is wonderful and funny and smart. She is a hottie and makes amazing and elaborate desserts.

As I mentioned, I am balding, with a bad shoulder from a stupid stunt I tried to do a couple of years ago, and I copastor New Life Christian Fellowship (NLCF), a wonderful and growing church in Blacksburg, Virginia, of around a thousand people who are strong and messed up at the same time. We have sent more church planters and missionaries out into the world than I even know about. We have started a number of social justice groups from within our church; people are really seeing that God wants them in the game. That is very exciting. At the same time, people can end up fighting over silly things and spend a lot of time doing silly things—myself included. Sometimes I wonder if I am capable of leading them.

I say all this because my life is great and not great all at the same time. Blessed and difficult. Sometimes I look around and wish I had a bigger house to park my broken-down car next to. Other times I look at videos about the Invisible Children of the Sudan and I feel guilty that I am not more grateful for what I already have.

My life was, overall, pretty normal, until April 16, 2007. That was the day "normal" changed.

PART I

The Questions Raised

1

A Surreal Day

I<small>T WAS A PRETTY QUIET DAY.</small> That seems such a clichéd way to start a book, but it is true. It was just very normal. I was in a coffee shop not far from Virginia Tech, from which I graduated some years ago. That day, mostly the regulars were there, mostly the normal discussions going on.

When word started coming out about a couple of shootings in Ambler Johnston, one of the larger residence halls on the campus, we weren't even sure anything was actually going on. You know how rumors can get started. So I didn't think there was much to it.

But we knew something was up when we heard the police sirens. Then word came in: one student killed and another wounded. Suddenly an endless stream of police cars sped past. We didn't know it at the time, but they were headed to Norris Hall, an academic building where Seung Hui Cho committed most of his killing.

As far as we knew at that point, the shooting was over. The

university had released a statement saying that a student had been killed and a young man was in custody. A terrible thing had happened, but at least that terrible thing was over. Normal life started picking up again.

Then we heard the police loudspeakers and someone in the coffee shop shouted, "Check the Web!" The front page of Virginia Tech's Web site said something like "There is a gunman on the loose; stay indoors and away from windows." Someone said the police had sealed the roads around campus.

Even then, it still didn't sink in. I was sitting three feet from massive floor-to-ceiling windows in that coffee shop, one block away from a campus that had a gunman who was definitely *not* in custody. Still, I felt sure they would get him. They always seem to. About an hour later the police reopened the roads, and at my wife's request, I went home. Neither one of us had a grasp on what had happened until I heard her in the next room start to cry as she watched the news coverage: "Oh no! Oh no! They are saying twenty students were killed!" I looked at the screen just as the newscaster confirmed it.

Emergency Measures

I met with my copastors about fifteen minutes later; I remember their faces looking a lot like mine. We were scared and stunned, but we had to get moving. We put some quick thoughts together and then had the rest of our staff come to my house to pray and plan.

We said some dazed prayers and as we were trying to get our feet under us, we turned to the coverage and watched in horror with the rest of the country and much of the world as the death count seemed to climb endlessly.

By this point it was getting very hard to get calls through overwhelmed cell towers. Cell phones, landlines, pagers, and IM were all overloaded as friends and family tried to make sure everyone they knew was safe. Facebook and MySpace groups were quickly put together and statuses were updated to say, "I'm okay!" or "I'm safe"—anything to get a reassuring word out.

Then the eerie math took over for those who should have heard from loved ones by then but had not. One girl later that night said to me, "You never imagine really praying that someone is too badly injured to answer their phone. But if my friend isn't injured, I'm too scared to even say what that means." We later found out that her friend had been killed.

As we were meeting with our whole staff in my family room, trying to focus on what needed to be done felt almost impossible. We were stunned and overwhelmed as we watched images on TVs and computer screens of the buildings many of us had taken classes in and the grass that all of us had walked and played on. But as those images went around the world they had some pretty horrific things scrolling under them. It is chilling to see places you walk by every day with captions like "22 confirmed dead," then "25 confirmed dead," or "Gunman believed to have shot himself." And all the time the body count kept rising. This tragedy was playing out about two miles from my house, but we watched it on CNN like everyone else.

I remember our team praying, crying a bit, arguing over what to do (very normal for us), and planning a response to a situation for which—we were all very aware—no playbook existed. All the while we wondered who from our church had made it home safely and who hadn't.

Then Larry King's people called my cell. It was decided that I would be the guy to handle most of the media stuff—I don't think for any more reason than that I can think quickly on my feet. I knew the reason the media wanted me on their shows: they wanted a spokesman for a God who didn't look as if he had handled things very well that day. I suddenly felt like a White House press secretary must feel when he or she walks into the pressroom to speak on behalf of an unpopular president. And honestly, it seemed as if God had some serious explaining to do.

They wanted a spokesman for a God who didn't look as if he had handled things very well that day.

We also went on planning a vigil for that night as well as for a time when Matt Rogers, one of our other pastors, would touch base with our key leaders on campus. We had to make sure they were all right and get them ready to walk the people they work with through this situation. Keep in mind that most of our leaders are early-twenty-somethings who themselves still weren't sure if all their friends and professors were safe. I can tell you that over the next several weeks they handled themselves like people with a lot more years of life experience under their belts.

We had absolutely no idea what we would do the next day. Our goal at this point was to just get through the night, find out who was safe and who wasn't, and try to adjust to this new crazy reality. I remember talking to three girl students the night of the sixteenth, and one confessed, "I don't know what to do. I am worried about my friend we cannot find, and I am also worried about my organic chemistry lab that is due in a couple of days!" That really desribed how we all felt. Normal and abnormal life had been fused together for all of us. People walked around town with the same look of utter disbelief on their faces.

Live with Larry King

About the time the vigil started, I drove into the area where all the media had set up shop. And as shocked and numbed—as frozen—as everyone from Blacksburg seemed to be, this place was the opposite. Every square inch of grass and asphalt was taken up with satellite trucks and the people who were running them. Literal fields of satellite dishes had sprouted from what had been an empty parking lot just that morning. All obscenely pointed up into the sky and to the myriad satellites waiting to receive signals with the latest nuggets of the misery we were living in.

As I walked into this swarm of instant news (or rather was swept into it), I found myself again in complete shock. Not only was I out of my element—I had no idea where my element even was.

**Not only was I out of my element—I had no idea
where my element even was.**

I remember seeing Geraldo walking very purposefully somewhere. I stood behind Brian Williams, who was waiting to get
some goldfish crackers, and was surprised he wasn't taller (he
always seemed taller on TV). But it really got weird when I
approached a media coordinator and asked where Larry King
was set up. At the very mention of that apparently magical
name, two small but surprisingly strong women yanked me
aside, introduced themselves with the speed of auctioneers, and
asked who I was and to spell my name. All the while they were
writing in their notebooks and sending e-mails on their Black-
Berry devices. I quickly learned that everyone in the media
business has a BlackBerry.

As I pulled away from them and started toward the location
where Larry's people were, a handler (for the media unsavvy,
that's someone in charge of getting you set up with a micro-
phone and in front of the cameras as fast as possible) found me
and started walking me over to the set. She said to her Blue-
tooth-equipped counterpart that she had "the pastor" and we
were on our way. I started to feel very naked without a Black-
Berry in my hand.

As we walked and hurdled our way to the set, she prepped
me. "Pastor"—I never could get anyone on a single show to just
call me Jim—"you will be on with Larry in New York and Dr.
Phil from Houston. Do you know Dr. Phil?"

I responded, "I have never heard of him."

She looked at me with a mixture of shock and what seemed to be amazement. And that is when I learned that newspeople don't have time for nervous/sarcastic humor from pastors at times like these. (Diane Sawyer would later remind me of that as well.) So I 'fessed up that I was aware of who Dr. Phil was.

She seemed comforted that I might not be as ignorant as she feared, told me that both Dr. Phil and Larry would be piped into my earpiece, and asked if I was ready to be fitted with one. Then they checked my sound levels, double-checked the spelling of my name, and off I went. Those satellite dishes shot my face and voice up into space and then in front of the eyes of anyone who cared to watch.

I had been pretty specific with the producers. I had no desire or need to be on any show; there were plenty of much more important things for me to do. The only reason I would do interviews was if I would have a chance to answer substantial questions of faith. What I was actually *able* to do in that first interview was say that I was in a coffee shop and that we were doing lots of things to help everyone cope. Then Dr. Phil took over.

I heard Larry announce a break and then heard a different voice say, "Pastor is done," and as quickly as I was attached, I was jettisoned.

As I drove back to the vigil, fuming at Larry, Dr. Phil, and a bit at God for the waste of my time, I got two calls from national morning shows asking me to be on. That's when I started feeling like the press secretary for God. But how do you explain what you don't fully understand? And why is it only during situations like this one that God seems to get center stage?

I started feeling like the press secretary for God.

A whole lot of people see the task of keeping the peace, or at least providing an acceptable level of protection, as one of God's key jobs. He even refers to himself as our protector in the Scriptures we read. And we tend to feel very safe here in the United States, especially in the mountains of Blacksburg, Virginia. Even more so here on Tech's campus.

At least we did until April 16.

What Is God Good For?

People start to wonder, *If God will let that kind of thing happen, then what is he good for?* In the interviews that followed the one with Larry King, questions like that came at me from not only *Anderson Cooper 360* and *Good Morning America*, but also from members of our church, people on campus, and friends and people around the country, even overseas. A fourteen-year-old from Topeka, Kansas, e-mailed *Good Morning America*, saying she didn't feel safe going to school. I was asked what I would say to her. That is a fun question to be asked on live TV.

Countless other questions came over the next days and months:

- "What does this say about God and your faith that is based on him being the most powerful, loving, present, and creative force in the universe?"
- "What do you think Jesus was doing on those final fateful moments just before and during Cho's rampage?"
- "Does this make you doubt God?"
- "Does this make you angry at him?"
- "Should we just fire God?"

I was being asked these questions at the same time I was asking God questions of my own.

The reality is that Seung Hui Cho tore a hole in our campus and community that day that was infinitely larger than the size of the bullets used to create it. It made people scared. It made them sad, and it made many confused and angry. Some of that anger had located itself at God's doorstep. As a result, it did seem as though I had something to answer for.

Some of that anger had located itself at God's doorstep.

You could almost feel the growing suspicion in people's questions and see it on their faces when they thought about God's part in all this. To them, this type of moment was no different from the entry of Dorothy, the Tin Woodsman, the Cowardly Lion, and the Scarecrow into the throne room of Oz. At first they were amazed and awed by all the sights and sounds the great Oz made. But a quick pull on a green curtain was all it took to reveal the truth. There was no almighty and great Oz at all, just a tiny man pulling levers and pushing buttons.

Did that day on the campus of Virginia Tech do the same? Did it show us the smallness of a God we used to think was so large? What about all the other horrid moments that are felt in our lives? Some are catastrophic and global; others are just as disastrous but more painfully personal.

What makes all this even worse is that bad things don't occur in a void, do they? Life still continues—both the good and the bad parts. In the two weeks following the shootings, both of my family's cars broke down. I distinctly remember having some direct, rather strong, conversations with God over that. If not problems with our cars, then with our kids, our classes, our money, our health, our relationships, you name it.

It was time to put my faith to the test: Was God really doing a good job?

Questions for Reflection and Discussion

1. When you think about God and the suffering we endure, what conclusions have you come to?
   - God is real, powerful, and loving and is waiting to end the suffering we all experience for some larger purpose.

- God is real and powerful but not caring or involved enough to step in. Rather, he is watching it unfold with us.
- God is real and cares about our suffering yet doesn't possess the actual power to meaningfully intervene in our suffering.
- God isn't real.

2. Why did you buy this book?

3. What are you hoping it will provide you in this discussion of whether or not God is doing his job sufficiently enough to earn our trust and allegiance?

2

You Never Forget Your First

I DATED THE WOMAN who is my wife now—her name is Tracy—for about three years before we got married. I have to be honest, most of the dates we went on blur together. Except for the first one.

I remember what she was wearing and what I was wearing. It was July 2. We went to the Smithsonian. I remember other firsts: how I wussily asked her out the first time, and the first time I told her I loved her.

Most of us remember the firsts. Not just the good ones either. I remember the first girl to break up with me. I remember the first time I realized I wasn't as cool as I thought I was. I remember the first time a close family member died. I remember the first time I was "detained" by the police. And I remember the first time God really let me down.

I mean *really* let me down. It wasn't the most difficult time that God and I have had, but, as they say, you never forget your first.

All of us probably know what it feels like to be disappointed by God. Sure, each of us has experienced that with different nuances: maybe a relationship fell apart, a loved one died or remains debilitated by physical or emotional wounds, economic downturns, violence. Sometimes it is just the everyday troubles that God could take away but doesn't.

All of us probably know what it feels like to be disappointed by God.

Here is my first.

I need to start by saying that I was a bit of a screwup growing up. Not all that bad, but if you were looking for a kid to place a bet on that he would grow up to have a superproductive adult life, I probably was not your guy.

That trend reversed itself in college: very strong grades, plans to get my PhD, and a professor who offered to walk me through the whole thing. Things were looking up, and my family could see it. I was no longer the screwup. Receiving respect where there previously wasn't much can be heady stuff.

But eventually I started to show cracks in my newfound "Jim has it together" persona. I became a follower of Jesus with about a year left at school. Then I wanted to go on a missions trip. Then, the kicker: I decided I would go into ministry full-time. No PhD. I wouldn't even go to seminary at first, but that wasn't the worst of it. I had to raise my own salary from individual people to fund what I was doing.

To much of my extended family this was decidedly not cool. And there it was: Jim was messing up again. And he had been doing so well.... But this time would be different, right? I felt sure it would be. This time, the reason I looked foolish was because I was responding to what God was leading me to do. It was a *huge* risk. Raising my own salary would be difficult at best, but God would show himself to be true, right? He would show himself to be powerful and real to members of my family who didn't think he was. Right?

This was such a dangerous choice for me; surely God would take me through it step-by-step.

Right?

I even went to one of the members of my extended family who was especially disappointed in my new career choice and told him I would show him that God was real. I had prayed a lot about this before I did it. I really felt God was leading me to draw a line in the sand, believe in him for something very specific, and tell this family member that I would not only finish my fund-raising (which he didn't believe I would), but I would finish it fast. I even set the date by which I would be finished. Then he called me parasitic for funding my ministry this way and told me I needed to grow up. Ahh, family.

Sure, lines like that hurt, but God would show himself through this. It was worth it. So my fund-raising began.

It All Falls Apart

I happened to see this person the week my line-in-the-sand date came. With a smirk on his face that I will always remember, he asked if I was finished yet. I told him I was at about 50 percent. He walked away with the same smirk he had coming in. God hadn't proved anything new to him at all.

I believed God could get my fund-raising finished up by a certain date. My faith was strong and I had worked hard. I did what I thought I was supposed to do: follow God way out on the limb. If God didn't come through, I would look foolish.

He didn't and I did.

**If God didn't come through, I would look foolish.
He didn't and I did.**

Not only that, it took my wife and I more than a year to finish our fund-raising, and we spent the next four or five years in deep financial difficulty. When she was pregnant with our first child, Tracy had only two maternity outfits, one of which was secondhand. I will never forget how when she broke her five-dollar sunglasses we both realized it would be months before we could afford to get her more. I remember the Wal-Mart brand spaghetti sauce that we could buy—it was three jars for five dollars, and we must have eaten that three or four days a week. At one point, we literally ran out of food and money, and it was going to be a few weeks until I got paid again.

Even payday wasn't very encouraging. With the way our funding worked—it was up to the supporters to make sure they sent in what they pledged, and on time—we got only as much as people sent—period. About a week before each payday I would go out to the mailbox and pull the statement that told us what we'd receive that month. Almost every single month for over a year, Tracy broke down and cried when I told her.

This wasn't how it was supposed to work. I had heard from God, I had turned from a much more respected path, I had endured embarrassment, and I had been dealing with extreme financial difficulty with no idea when it would end. Needless to say, I was confused, and then I started to get fed up.

I would go out to a hill behind our house. It was fairly remote and no one could hear me when I was there. I went there almost every single day for months. I went to that hill to scream at God. I was so angry and hurt. I felt betrayed and lied to. I even had a big stick that I kept up on one of the hills that I pounded into the ground until I tired out. The pressure seemed unrelenting.

I went to that hill to scream at God.

That made it tough. Knowing when something will be over makes even great difficulty at least a bit more bearable. Not knowing adds to the pain even more. But that wasn't the worst part.

The worst part was that I felt tricked by God. Remember my little attempt to show God was real by declaring that I would finish my fund-raising by a certain point? Sure, maybe my heart wasn't completely right in that, but for the most part it was. Granted, maybe I didn't do everything I could have on my end to finish, but I did a whole lot. Maybe I didn't really hear God say that was what I should do, but I thought I had. I didn't know that I was running headlong into a huge embarrassment.

But God knew. That was the truly tough part. He knew the whole time as I was walking out on that limb that it would crack under my weight with everyone watching. He knew that, once again, I would publicly fail. That I—and by this point, my wife and son along with me—would struggle when we could be thriving. That I would be embarrassed and look foolish to people whose opinions mattered.

That wasn't the first time I felt as if I'd had the rug pulled out from under me. But that was the first time I looked to God for help as I pulled myself up, and, instead of receiving it, I saw the rug tassels sticking out from between his fingers.

Raw and Real

As I said, there just always seems to be something about the first time. Once you have felt like that toward God, you can see it in other people's faces when they are frustrated too. It's as if you have some sort of radar. And even years after my first tough season with God, I still notice that look: confusion, even fear. And after one of our gatherings last year, I noticed it very clearly on the face of a girl I had never met before.

She looked pretty much like all the others around her, in her late teens or early twenties, long hair, wearing jeans and a T-shirt. Kind of hesitant, she was hanging on the edge of the group of people I was talking to after one of our gatherings. I kept trying to catch her eye to see if she would come into the circle, but every time she saw me look at her, her eyes shot back down to the ground. So once I finished talking with the people there, I went over to her, introduced myself, and asked how she was doing.

"Well, that is kind of why I am here, I guess. . . . You are probably pretty busy so this is really no big deal."

I told her that it seemed as though she wanted to talk about something and maybe we could just sit for a minute. If she still felt her issue was not a big deal, then that would be fine. She agreed.

When we sat, it was as if a lever had been thrown and everything started to pour out. "Why would he let something like this happen? Things were just beginning to settle down. Life was starting to get good—and now this."

Life was starting to get good—and now this.

For about half an hour she expressed anger, fear, frustration, and above everything else, confusion. At first every other sentence was qualified with "This is not usually how I am" or "I felt like you would understand and not judge me," but after a bit that stopped and she just let it all out, raw and real and completely understandable. She was confused and angry. And it all made sense.

As one of the pastors of a large church that is made up primarily of people in their late teens to somewhere in their forties, it is normal for people to want to talk to me, and the questions this young person was struggling with were normal too. But she wasn't talking about a guy she was dating, a roommate who would never do the dishes, or a spouse she feared was losing interest in her.

The "he" she was referring to was God. And the "it" she mentioned was April 16, a day that has been just as surely redefined in our common understanding in the Virginia Tech community as September 11 has to our entire country.

The shootings that occurred that day happened in a small university town, one of the last places you would ever think something like that would happen. There were thirty-two dead plus the gunman, who, in a last definitive and cowardly gesture, turned the gun on himself, ensuring that the killing would stop, but robbing so many of the justice important to the healing process. And the questions that have been reverberating through many people's heads are easily stated, but very difficult to answer honestly or satisfactorily.

- "Why?"
- "How could this happen?"
- "Why didn't you do something, God?"

Why did God let something like this happen? Was it random violence, and we happened to be on the receiving end? Was God trying to make a point and using our university as the illustration? If so, what possible point could there be in violence that seems without reason? What possible cause could God further by seeing twenty-eight students and four professors killed? They were normal people living their normal lives, going to class or teaching. It was just regular life for them.

Or was Friedrich Nietzsche right about faith when he said it was "not wanting to know what is true"?

Worldwide Suffering

The problem with following God meaningfully in a world where such horrific violence occurs daily is a big one. We cannot just shove our heads in the sand and ignore the tough questions that life in our world raises; neither do we want to walk away from God if he is real. We are intelligent and well-informed people, and that can make resolution tough. We not only know that tragedy is occurring in Darfur, but we have seen close-ups of children displaced, women raped. These images are etched into our brains, and we cannot and should not act as if they aren't.

For me two haunting images come to mind that represent unacceptable suffering. One is of a blind grandmother literally crawling in the sand away from her life. Her family had all been murdered, her house burned to the ground, and following her was her three-year-old grandson, wide-eyed with shock and fear. She was crawling in darkness away from darkness. I don't think that image will ever leave me.

Another is of a man I learned was once a medical student in

South Africa. Like an agonizingly high percentage of the population in that country, he contracted HIV, which eventually developed into full-blown AIDS. He lost his job, worked for a while as a street vendor, and lived in a homeless camp until his AIDS status was discovered. He was forced to leave the camp and was found dead after a night of freezing temperatures, wearing only tattered clothes and huddled next to a woodpile under a blue tarp.

Not only are we aware that drought conditions are threatening farmers' livelihoods all across the country, but we can go onto the Web and see how little they have to sell their farms for. Children who live within two hundred miles of my house are so immersed in poverty that their extraction seems practically impossible...while I get offer after offer for credit cards. It isn't just that it is wrong, but our world can be so bitterly unfair. And we aren't just aware that shootings occurred at this place called Blacksburg, but we all have seen Seung Hui Cho in the pictures and heard his angry ramblings included in the media packet he mailed off during the break he took in the killings.

So we know what is going on, and we cannot just ignore it. But how do we handle it? No longer can we claim ignorance of the pain in the world. In Blacksburg the collision with that terrible violence only increased our awareness. The violence that much of the world has needed to contend with for hundreds of years finally found its way to our door.

And as we try to make some modicum of sense of this, questions linger in the air: Is God really up to the job of being God in our world today? How's he doing at it? How was he doing at it on April 16, 2007, or any of the other days where pain seems to rain down on us? And the questions that often come right after it are: Why do we have him there—habit? Maybe blind hope that someone is watching things for us? Could Aldous Huxley have been right when he said, "All gods are homemade, and it is we who pull their strings, and so, give them the power to pull ours"? Could all this God-talk just be some concoction that was started with the best of intentions but has now outlived its usefulness?

Is God really up to the job of being God in our world today?

Maybe our temptation amid the frustration we feel is to fly over these issues. Set them aside and move on to more pressing matters. To some, asking these questions of God may even seem wrong—inappropriate. But our world doesn't afford us the luxury of pushing them aside, does it? If our faith is to be real and meaningful, we must be willing to enter into some necessary discussions that can be hurtful and confusing.

We have to be able to go there. Any God who can handle the job of being God in our world today must be able to handle those questions.

But we have to deal with something else first.

What I Believe, Simply Stated

Let me lay my cards on the table. I am a follower of Jesus Christ. I would say "Christian," but a whole lot of baggage goes with that term. Hence I prefer "follower of Jesus." I believe he is the part of God who came down to earth to help us with an infection that our rebellion against God had created; the word the Bible uses for this is *sin*. I think Jesus did something for me that neither I nor anyone else on the planet could do—he saved me from sin.

This isn't all I believe about God, just the tip of the iceberg really, but it is the part that matters the most now. I also think that the Bible is a highly accurate depiction of what God has been up to in our world and how we have responded to him over time.

I have not always believed these things—and that matters. For the bulk of my life, I didn't believe in Jesus. I used to think Christianity was the default belief for Americans who didn't really question their world and wanted or needed a reason to behave the way they should. I thought the Bible was a bit like Aesop's fables.

Remember those? Who wouldn't do well to think through the fable of the fox and the crow or the ugly duckling? It doesn't matter a bit if Aesop lived around twenty-six hundred years ago. His fables share great proverbial wisdom that we ignore at our own peril, even today. We can choose to pay attention and learn that not everyone who compliments us has our best in mind, or we can naively learn that lesson the hard way. We would do well to heed his words. But that's just the point, isn't it? *We can choose.* Aesop makes no claim of authority in our lives. He was an ancient Greek slave and storyteller. He shared great truths about life you could heed if you wanted to or ignore.

But unlike Aesop's fables, the Scriptures are more than helpful hints and nice ideas; I see them as God's words to us that describe him, the world we live in, and us as well. That realization hasn't blinded me to the things going on in this world that make believing deeply in God difficult. While I do believe in the reality of Jesus, I don't want to ignore the overwhelming suffering around me. Actually, my faith in Jesus has led me to look at the world's suffering much more closely. But some things in the Bible are hard for me to understand, and other things even make me angry at times. Just like the world I live in.

Some things in the Bible are hard for me to understand, and other things even make me angry at times. Just like the world I live in.

So God and I still have some problems. Sometimes I am confused or angry, sometimes blindingly happy, usually somewhere in between.

As I said, I define Scripture as an account that describes who God is revealing himself to be. As with a testimony in court, I trust it. But I haven't always felt the Bible's testimony was reliable, and I am sure some who are reading this still wonder. Your wondering matters. Because even if there really is a God (which

I wasn't sure of for twenty-one years of my life), if the Bible isn't accurate in how it talks about him, it should be discarded, or at least not trusted in and of itself.

I cannot relay everything I had to wrestle with in my years of deliberation over whether I could really trust this old book. I can tell you that *Another Evidence That Demands a Verdict* by Josh McDowell, *The Case for Christ* by Lee Strobel, *Mere Christianity* by C. S. Lewis, and more recently *Simply Christian* by N. T. Wright, among others, were very helpful to me in my processing of everything. They are full of research and facts you can check for yourself (I did) that go beyond mere opinion.

I also continue to think through these issues. I have read most of the more recently published books written by authors who claim the Scriptures are not trustworthy and the God those Scriptures point to isn't really there. Some of them are very well written and the authors come from solid backgrounds. But in every case, as I read the arguments against either the historic nature of the Scriptures, the debate made by those that follow them, or the ability to trust the Scriptures we now have, I continue to see the weaknesses in the arguments posed by those authors. All this to say that I am not someone who has put his head in the sand and keeps repeating "I hope this is right; I hope this is right." I think through these issues deeply and continue to trust the Scriptures to be a faithful guide to a very loving and real God.

You may also notice that sometimes I refer to God as *God,* other times as *God the Father, God the Son,* or *God the Holy Spirit.* I will also refer to God as *Jesus* or *Holy Spirit.* I will get into this more later, but the reason for this is that I hold to the view that these are all God—not separate gods that come together on the same team, but rather different parts of God that at times function distinctly and at other times function wholly. I realize this can be confusing.

So, that is where I stand. I didn't get there quickly, and while I recognize that just my saying I have become sufficiently convinced of the Scriptures' accuracy won't be enough for some of you, we have to start somewhere, right? So, now you know where I am coming from.

Should God Be Fired?

So, how do we begin sorting out this question of whether or not God should be fired? Maybe we could start to get his version of how we have found ourselves here. And what he thinks qualifies him for the job. Like any reporter covering a story, any detective interviewing a witness, or any human resources department employee dealing with an issue between workers would say . . .

Let's start at the beginning.

First, God claims he is the founder of everything. We need to go way back in time to hear the story, but God relays it to us through Moses like this: When God got started creating the universe and the earth as part of it, there was nothing but him anywhere. Everything else was dark and formless until he got going and pulled everything into existence (Genesis 1:1–2). In twenty-seven verses, and over some period of time, we as humans came on the scene. God created us. The Scriptures say that we carry his image; we bear his likeness (Genesis 1:27).

But just because he was here first, are we stuck with him? Is the world we live in really just like some gigantic trade union where God is in charge of us because he has the most seniority? Do our concerns about him not matter because he has some sort of cosmic dibs? Is that enough of a reason to follow him?

Not anymore. We now live in a world laden with information that comes at us with dizzying speeds. We have access to live coverage of a baby Panda sneezing in Beijing, a World's Strongest Man competition (you should really watch one of those if you haven't), pictures of natural and man-made atrocities like the ones I mentioned before, or the shootings at a seemingly safe university in Virginia all at once. Instant access, all the time.

That kind of accessibility changes the landscape a bit. People know what is going on around the globe in real time. The problems of the world are brought to us instantly in high-def and can be saved on our DVRs. And the more we know, the faster the questions about God's performance come. Instantaneous, time-stamped pain and suffering are brought to us so clearly that we not only know the woman we are watching has been crying, we can see the individual rivulets of mascara and tears on her face.

Remember now, this is really a pretty recent phenomenon. This speed of information transmission and clarity are very new to us. Prior to this point in our human history, if you weren't in the area when the newsworthy event happened, it could take weeks, or months in the case of global news, before you heard

about it. This newfound access and immersion into the pain of
the entire planet has changed us.

Sympathy Cringes

In their very compelling study, "A Unifying View of the Basis
of Social Cognition," Vittorio Gallese, Christian Keysers, and
Giacomo Rizzolatti examined one of the most intriguing devel-
opments in neurophysiology. Essentially they explored the
impact that mirror neurons have on us. While still far from a
mapped system, these neurons' presence would seem to bridge
the gap between human beings. Let me explain what mirror
neurons do.

Simply put, whenever we get poked with a pin, we have a
certain neurological response that allows us to register the pain
and to move away from it. This is nothing new. But Gallese,
Keysers, and Rizzolatti looked at a new wrinkle. They found that
when we observe someone *else* getting poked by a pin, certain
components of our neurological systems—mirror neurons—
actually fire as if we had been poked ourselves.[1] What that
means is that when we see someone get poked and cringe, we
are not just cringing out of empathy based on our experience of
pain in the past, but, in some manner, our brains are registering
that we are experiencing the pain as well. Certainly to a lesser
degree, but we have some communal experience of what we see.
If I may: our brains know that we aren't being poked ourselves,
but only partly.

Unless there is something more to all this, then our only concern would be to avert our eyes from people when they get pricked with a pin, and we should be fine. But these neurons present a much broader potential implication. They say that we connect with the pain we see around us. Again, not just empathetically. We don't just understand others are experiencing difficulty and feel badly for them; we understand that they are experiencing difficulty and our bodies register that as if *we* actually were experiencing difficulty as well. So it would appear we are much more deeply connected to the suffering we see everywhere than we may have thought. Their pain is registered, to a smaller degree, as ours.

So, our exposure to the suffering of those around us impacts us psychologically and, though to a lesser extent, physically. The pain we see as a woman talks about her marriage unfolding, the fear we saw on Elian Gonzales's face as the home he was staying in was stormed by armed police officers, the anger we feel when we watch Sudanese warlords explain why they are right in their views of their enemies, the twisting pain etched in the faces of Madeleine McCann's parents as they try to find their daughter, all the while carrying around her favorite pink elephant: all gets mixed in with the pain we have personally suffered, the loss of loved ones, the breakup of relationships, the difficulty of financial downturns, a disability that has become a part of our lives, or an illness. This is our everyday reality. This is where we live, and many times it feels as if it doesn't line up with a world that has God looking over it and keeping things in check.

It feels as if his work might be slipping a bit. So we have questions.

**It feels as if his work might be slipping a bit.
So we have questions.**

Pain Waves

There is a strange thing about enduring something as massive and terrible as we did here at Virginia Tech. It doesn't hit you all at once. The full impact comes to you more in waves.

One place it hit me was at the memorial of Caitlin Hammaren, one of the shooting victims who had visited our church. I was sitting toward the back and watched the crowd file in. Caitlin's childhood and college friends were there, as were her boyfriend and her sorority sisters. One after another, they shared their pain with all of us.

I thought about her parents. I cannot possibly understand the loss that Caitlin's parents must have been feeling. No more Thanksgiving and Christmas traditions to share. The goofy gifts and inside jokes. The one-on-one times with her as they continued to watch her grow. They wouldn't be able to celebrate with her and watch her receive the degree that she had worked so hard to earn. No waiting anxiously to hear about her first real job or helping her decorate her first apartment. Her father couldn't walk her down the aisle at her wedding. Her mother couldn't calm her nerves through her first pregnancy. No grand-children. She was their only child. All that was gone.

All that pain, and this was in just one of the memorials and funerals that were held almost every day for the next few weeks. The sense of loss and pain and unfairness of it all was suffocating.

So many other parents would be grieving, not just the loss of their children, but the loss of their futures with those children. Children would be grieving the loss of their futures with par-ents and grandparents who would never come home again.

More hit me again at the beginning of the next school year. The Drillfield was again filled with people at the dedication of a memorial to the victims. A representative for each victim stood in a semicircle to receive a commemorative piece of stone. A bell was rung and then, one by one, the representatives returned to the tent where they were seated.

What was so overwhelming was the sheer number of times that bell had to toll. And each person who walked back to the shade of the tent that afternoon represented who knows how many people who were still experiencing indescribable pain. How can you wrap your mind around that amount of suffering?

Add to that the difficulty that develops so often in relation-ships and families and groups as they seek to deal with this kind of terrible loss. Families will be torn apart by this. People will carry wounds that they won't always see or understand but will be impacted by for the rest of their lives.

I remember just being overwhelmed with sadness—then anger. First at Cho for inflicting this on us, then at the world for being a place where such evil resides, and then at God for not keeping things under control.

This from just one terrible day in Blacksburg, Virginia.

Each of us is watching this play out with greater signal strength than ever. Watching it all, and whether we realize it or not, we aren't just watching, we are experiencing a bit of it as our own. And even more, we are simultaneously standing in line, waiting for the pain this world releases to find its way to us.

Our concerns are real. The terrible things we have seen in our world are real. And the questions it all produces are real.

We all have some questions for God.

We all have had our firsts with God. Whether or not you follow him personally, you have been hurt by the world he presides over. We have our history of pain and confusion, and it must be dealt with to move forward. To get closer to God, the list must come out and be looked at.

We have our history of pain and confusion, and it must be dealt with to move forward.

Questions for Reflection and Discussion

1. When was the first time God really let you down?

2. In reflection, what reasons do you feel he might have had for doing that?

3. To you, what is the purpose of faith in Jesus as our Messiah?

4. What are some of the scenes of suffering you have experienced personally or heard about that have most impacted you? What do those scenes do to your faith in God?

5. How do you view the Scriptures of the Old and New Testaments? What process did you go through to reach that conclusion?

6. Have you noticed the discussed effect of mirror neurons on you personally? If so, describe what that was like.

3

The Questions Are as Old as Time

To EXAMINE PART OF THE WORLD'S HISTORY with pain, we can look at the great exchange between a guy named Gideon and an angel of God in the Old Testament book of Judges. In it we see that people for thousands of years have struggled with the breakdown between what they think our world should look like if God is paying attention and the one we live in. God wanted to have a conversation with Gideon. He had a job for him. Gideon was about to become part of something very large; he just didn't know it yet.

Here is what was going on at the time: a neighboring group of people called the Midianites were harassing Israel. By *harassing*, I mean that for six years the Midianites and others had pushed the Israelites to the brink of starvation.

The Israelites were primarily an agricultural people with several crop rotations throughout the year as well as livestock. Both crops and livestock are tough to hide should you need to. And they needed to.

What the Midianites did was wait until the Israelites' crops were ready for harvest and their livestock had given birth. Then they would descend on the Israelites. The best way the author of Judges could describe how many Midianites would descend on Gideon's people was to liken them to locusts. If you have ever experienced a full-on locust assault, you get how it can be. I've witnessed a couple. For several days the noise is so loud you cannot escape it; the locusts fly around in clouds that can literally darken the sky. During one locust storm, the air was so thick with them that our dog would jump up and catch two or three in his mouth (and our dog couldn't catch anything!). When they left, they took about everything that was green with them.

The author says the Midianites ravaged the land and the Israelites were desperately impoverished by it (Judges 6:5–6). Just imagine going through that. All your livestock has been taken. You planted some crops where you could in the hope that the Midianites would grow bored with you and maybe leave you alone.

Then, right about harvesttime you would see it, far off at first, then slowly and cruelly growing nearer and larger in size. You hope it is nothing, just dust kicked up by one of the windstorms that often descend on your part of the world. Then, at some point, you would be able to tell exactly what it was. The Midianites hadn't forgotten you at all. They were on their way back. And once again they would take everything you had, things you needed to survive, for no reason other than that they wanted to and your people weren't strong enough to stop them.

Now, let's try something here. As I write this I am sitting in a coffee shop with some of that generic coffee-shop jazz playing in the background. You may be sitting in another coffee shop, hearing much of the same. Or maybe you are at home in your favorite chair, or on a plane. . . . Let's try to forget for a bit where we are and what is going on around us. Let's try to imagine that we are Israelites ourselves, that we are experiencing what Gideon and his people experienced.

Gideon wasn't fictional, nor was what he and his people went through. If you had been living then, you wouldn't have the privilege of thinking, *That sounds terrible*, and then moving on. For the people of Gideon's time, that dust cloud symbolized unavoidable tragedy to come.

These events didn't just mean things would get a bit harder—inconvenient—for a while, but rather that some of the people you loved probably wouldn't survive. It meant the food your kids needed to live—not to thrive, mind you, just to *live*—wouldn't be there. It meant that you had two main choices.

Neither was any good.

You could stand your ground and defy the Midianites, choose not to let them take your food and your dignity with it. If you did that, you would almost certainly be killed. The Midianites didn't get their savage reputation by letting people deny them what they had the power to take. And if you did that, where would your family be then? You would be dead and your family *still* wouldn't have enough food.

So you could choose the other option: do nothing and try

to just survive the annual mini-invasion. Let the locusts eat and then hope they will leave when they have taken all they can.

Both were soul-crushing options.

You know how mad you and I can get when someone cuts us off in traffic and acts as if it is our fault? You know how we feel when people skip ahead of us in line or blame us for their mistakes? We don't swallow injustice well, especially injustice directed at us. What the Israelites faced was in a whole different league. You can tell they were frustrated and angry.

At the Midianites... and at God.

We don't swallow injustice well, especially injustice directed at us.

Enter Gideon

Finally it got bad enough that the Israelites, the people of God, turned back to him and asked for help. It took six years of oppression and starvation for them to see that they needed God to survive.

So, up comes this angel from God to speak with Gideon, who is trying to thresh some wheat in a winepress—not the place you want to do your threshing. Admittedly, my firsthand experience with threshing is pretty nonexistent, but I get the idea. You gently toss the grain and the stalk and everything into the air. The stalk and the rest of the waste fly away, and the grain, being just a bit heavier, falls down. Then you can collect the grains and use them for food. You can also lay out the wheat to be threshed and have it stomped or beaten with a flail. Either way, you will do well to get some wind around it. You want to get rid of the stalk and keep the grain.

But here is our soon-to-be-hero, in a winepress. Threshing. Hiding.

And by the looks of it, he's angry.

This being approaches Gideon and it would seem that at first Gideon doesn't realize it is an angel. The angel says, "Mighty hero, the LORD is with you!" (Judges 6:12 NLT).

We cannot be sure of the tone in Gideon's voice, but we do know what he said and it seems he didn't take the angel very seriously: "If the LORD is with us, why has all this happened to us? And where are all the miracles our ancestors told us about? Didn't they say, 'The LORD brought us up out of Egypt'? But now the LORD has abandoned us and handed us over to the Midianites" (6:13 NLT).

Gideon has questions—and not ones that are ethereal and disconnected from his life. His questions are born out of his life, his personal experience. Sure, you can tell he understands what he has been told about his people's life with God. God had done some cool things . . . in the past. But now, Gideon has issues with God. He feels abandoned. It would seem that Gideon didn't think God was doing a very good job anymore.

**Gideon didn't think God was doing a very good job
anymore.**

For those of us who have read the story, we know what is
coming. We can hear the theme music from *Rocky* playing in
the background, quietly at first, but then growing louder and
louder. We know that the Midianites have a big-time whup-
ping coming straight at them. God is going to do something so
remarkable it will change the direction of Gideon's life and put
an end to the Midianites' abuse. But you can tell pretty quickly
that Gideon isn't hearing the music. Not at all.

To him, this is just another day of a life that really wasn't
worth living. For all Gideon knows, this angel is taunting him.
So, no "Eye of the Tiger." Just questions, anger, doubt. Possibly
even complete disbelief, but definitely not excitement.

Sound familiar? To me it does. Sure, the antagonizers are
different, but then they always are. Take the emotion that is
just like ours, the confusion that is just like ours, mix in some
anger, some frustration, and some terrible specifics, and there
you have it: another person with real questions about how God
is handling the world he is living in.

This account is fascinating and full of amazing indications
of God's very real power that was shown because a man was
willing to just say yes. For the full account take a look at Judges
6–8. You will see God being very powerful and loving and at
times, well, a bit weird. But very cool stuff happened during

Gideon's life, to be sure! And we find out very quickly in the Bible that it wasn't just the normal people who had a hard time with God, but the leaders too. The impressive ones, the dynamos, had a hard time as well.

The Confused Father of a Nation Wrestles with Doubt

People with questions and frustrations go back further than Gideon. Abraham, several hundred years earlier, seemed to have a hard time with God's methods too. Abraham was the guy from whom God promised to bring the entire Israelite nation. That is quite a promise. Essentially God said he was going to bless Abraham and Sarah's family. They would have a lot of kids, those kids would have a lot of kids, and so on. Eventually, an entire nation would form.

Abraham seemed to have a hard time with God's methods too.

But there were a couple of big problems. When God made that promise, Abraham and Sarah were old and known to be barren. And that was not copasetic back then. In Abraham's day, if a couple didn't have children, their financial security during old age was in jeopardy! There were no 401(k)s, just the hope that you would have 401 kids. Children were the retirement plan and their support was crucial. But that wasn't the only thing that came with infertility then. There would have also been the understandable sadness of not having kids of their own. Some very good friends of mine struggle with infertility and their suffering is significant. But back in Abraham and Sarah's day, another issue made it even worse. It meant that those around you would wonder whether you were being punished by God. Many saw childlessness as divine judgment.

So, even though Abraham was a very successful businessman and seemed to have a great marriage to Sarah, his life would have been a bit like the 756th ball that Barry Bonds rocketed over the fence to become the Major League's new home-run king. (A great achievement, but tainted by the question of his possible steroid use. Unless that is put away, people will always add a "but" after listing Bonds's accomplishments.) It would have been very much like that for Abraham and Sarah.

Then God spoke and made a crazy promise to this old barren couple. They would not only have a child, but Abe's offspring would outnumber the sands on the shore and he would be the father of a nation of God's people.

We cannot know this for sure, but I would be willing to bet that the tent flaps were billowing that night! And then they waited for Sarah to show signs of pregnancy...for years. They waited and waited for this baby who would signal the start of the fulfillment of a mind-blowing promise God had made. As the years passed, God never rescinded his promise, but it sure wasn't looking as if much was going to happen either. Over time, Abraham stopped trusting that God knew what he was doing and got scared. Eventually he lost heart that God would give him any children at all, much less enough to start a nation.

He and Sarah took things into their own hands and decided Abraham should have sex with one of Sarah's servants. A common practice at the time, but not exactly what God had in mind!

Once again, let's not look at this through our eyes. Our eyes don't matter here; Abraham's and Sarah's do. They had an idea of how God would handle the fulfillment of what seemed to be a straightforward promise. And nothing happened. For a very long time—years, even—he left them swinging . . . another couple asking questions about God's performance. (Eventually God fulfilled his promise—but here we are concerned with the couple's questions and anxiety while they waited.)

The Old and New Testaments seem to be full of people who both interacted with God and were also frustrated with the way he handled the world they were in. Their world, our same concerns. Their contexts, our same questions.

- "Why this way, God?"
- "Why haven't you done more?"
- "Why didn't you step in sooner, or more decisively?"
- "Why didn't you keep this from happening?"
- "Why couldn't you have made sure this did happen?"
- "Are you really up to your job anymore?"

Today, we don't toss these questions around as a matter of curiosity or for the intellectual challenge of it. Our faith, at least any real, dynamic form of it, depends on our coming to some conclusions. For me, questions have been a regular part of my personal relationship with Jesus. Prior to the shootings, two or three people came each month to discuss these questions. Now I've stopped counting; they just keep coming. And they have to. We cannot divert our attention as easily as some might. We live where the shootings happened, and, for many, their lives have been spared but their faith is on the line.

If this sounds like you, keep reading.

Questions for Reflection and Discussion

1. What parts of Gideon's story (Judges 6–8) resonate with you?
   - his fearful life prior to God's messenger speaking with him
   - his lack of awareness that God was speaking to him through the messenger
   - his awareness that God *had* done great things for the Israelites, but, since he hadn't experienced any of those personally, he doubted God would do them anymore
   - Gideon's anger at God for how his life had gone

2. If you were in Gideon's position, do you think you would have followed what God was calling you to do? What in your life demonstrates this?

3. What about Abraham's story resonates with you? Has

God ever appeared to have left you hanging the way he seemed to do to Abraham and Sarah?

4. When you face the level of confusion and frustration that Abraham and Sarah must have been feeling, how quickly does your trust in God give out?

5. Even if you are frustrated with the way God works with people in the Old and New Testaments, do you appreciate the honesty that is used to describe life with him?

PART II

Judging God

4

How Could He?

I SIT HERE WATCHING a light rainfall. The grass everywhere is greener as a result; the flowers stand up taller. We really needed it. A little more would have been even better.

During the writing of this book, I learned that the people of Myanmar had experienced disaster because too much water came roaring at them. Cyclone Nargis was expected to be a very bad one. Its trajectory had been tracked since the end of April and most expected it to take the track that storms in this region tend to, toward Bangladesh or Myanmar's mountainous northern region. This size of storm was never good, but at least it would hit in a fairly unpopulated region.

Only this one didn't go where expected. It hooked around and turned eastward. The storm headed for the Irrawaddy region, where most of the people live. Myanmar is one of the poorest countries in the world, and the people have almost no ability to handle or heal from that scale of devastation.

On May 2, 2008, a wall of water twelve feet high surged in front of 120 mph winds and shot more than twenty-five miles inland. Seven large townships experienced the loss of 95 percent of their buildings and structures. Early death toll estimates were at fifty thousand. The before-and-after satellite imagery made you think it must not be the same place.[1]

All because of an uncharacteristic hard eastern hook. It just seems as though God could have seen that one coming.

The news from Myanmar was soon replaced on May 12, 2008, by news that China had experienced an earthquake that was listed at 7.8 on the Richter scale. It hit central China's Sichuan region, and early estimates were that ten thousand may have died. That number would later rise to over sixty-five thousand, and it would become the nineteenth most deadly earthquake of all time. Cranes frantically tried to remove the remnants of a shattered school that had collapsed on nine hundred students. In the midst of the devastation they were already feeling, Chinese parents had to leave their crushed homes and businesses and wait for the cranes to do their work, wondering if the sounds of crying they heard in the rubble could possibly be from their children—or if their voices had been silenced forever.[2]

Can you imagine what it must be like to have your children crying in pain and fear as the best possible outcome?

Can you imagine what it must be like to have your children crying in pain and fear as the best possible outcome?

These are big deals. Not that suffering on a smaller scale is better—absolutely not. But the argument could be made that disaster of this proportion could be more easily spotted. Maybe the suffering of an individual could slip through the cracks— unintended certainly, but understandable. But gigantic earth- quakes, massive cyclones, and mass death? If you are someone with the capacity to stop this level of disaster and you do not— you start to look very bad.

If you are someone with the capacity to stop this level of disaster and you do not—you start to look very bad.

Defending God

The *Las Vegas Review-Journal* reported:

> The crime scene photos of Sierra Tisdale show a lifeless, emaciated baby with curly dark hair in a soiled crib, with feces oozing from every corner of her unchanged diaper.
> At the time of the child's 2002 death from starvation, the case was considered one of the worst examples of child neglect in Clark County in recent memory.[3]

I am a pastor, and one of people's spiritual expectations is that I am able to forgive when I am—or someone else is— wronged. I am supposed to be peaceable and self-controlled, among so many other things. But if I am honest, when I read about Sierra Tisdale, dying with "feces oozing from every corner of her unchanged diaper," grace isn't what I feel first.

We ask ourselves, What could possess a mother to allow such a horrific death for her little girl? Sure, Sophia Mendoza was under tremendous pressure: she was nineteen, had five kids and an abusive boyfriend, and "there were indications that [she] used methamphetamine."[4] Not a recipe for a happy home life, to be sure, but at a certain point, excuses simply fail.

Those facts cannot push away the truth that Sophia went out to lunch to celebrate her birthday the same day little Sierra was found to have been dead about twenty-four hours.

In the same house, a wax apple was found to have bite marks in it.

That much neglect is just too much.

To some, God is guilty of similar levels of neglect and abuse. The specifics are different, but the lack of care is the same. To some, God's explanations aren't important—in much the same way that many would say that Sophia's aren't. Many people aren't looking for the deeper issue, the bigger picture. The facts are what they are: Sophia created a child and then let that child slowly, and probably painfully, die. Enough said.

Just imagine a friend comes up and starts talking to you about Sophia Mendoza. Let's say he doesn't just bring her up, he talks about the great things she had done. As he talks about Sophia's selfless acts, he sees the look of disbelief on your face. He responds with a knowing smile and says, "I get this all the time. You are missing the point! She is really a wonderful woman!" Then he describes to you how you should follow Sophia's example in your life!

The problem is that you don't think you have missed anything at all. To some, the good things someone (or God) might do simply don't make the bad go away.

In *The God Delusion*, Richard Dawkins describes God in even worse terms than most convicted felons have been saddled with:

> The God of the Old Testament is arguably the most unpleasant character in all fiction: jealous and proud of it; a petty, unjust, unforgiving control-freak; a vindictive, bloodthirsty ethnic cleanser; a misogynistic, homophobic, racist, infanticidal, genocidal, filicidal, pestilential, megalomaniacal, sadomasochistic, capriciously malevolent bully.[5]

Yikes. C'mon, Richard. Tell us what you really think!

Tough words, but ones that we who follow God cannot throw away just because we have a different conclusion. The reality of the world we live in is that there are many instances in which God can seem to deserve having one or more of these descriptions applied to him. Maybe not "capriciously malevolent bully"—but on the other hand, if we are honest, do we always think of him as "all-loving and all-good"?

A Tree Is Known by Its Fruit

In the account of Jesus' life written by Luke, Jesus was quoted as saying that essentially you identify a tree by the fruit that grows on it. An apple tree may look like most other trees until it begins to grow apples. It doesn't become a foundationally different tree once the apples start growing; you are just able to see what type of tree it was the whole time.

In Luke 6:45, Jesus is referring to the nature and status of the hearts of the people around him: "The good man brings good things out of the good stored up in his heart, and the evil man brings evil things out of the evil stored up in his heart." Jesus puts his finger right on the issue when he adds, "For out of the overflow of his heart his mouth speaks" (NIV). Simply put, you cannot hide what is in your heart because what you do and say will reflect it. Your words and actions show what is inside.

To struggle with what God seems either to be producing or allowing doesn't seem so far out of bounds. If we are judged by what happens in our lives, should not God be judged the same way? For too long, this has been deemed an inappropriate question. But it shouldn't be. If Jesus, who was God, told us that our actions would reveal what is going on in our hearts, shouldn't God be expected and able to stand up to the same scrutiny?

If we are judged by what happens in our lives, should not God be judged the same way?

Yes, but perhaps we have missed something else.

We Don't Always Get What We Don't Get

I just saw a two-year-old named Trent run head-first into a clear glass door. He bumped his head and bounced right off. Once he got up, his dad helped him to stop crying and then explained in great two-year-old-ese (I know because I am fluent) that he shouldn't run like that at the door or he could get hurt. The newly enlightened Trent then nodded his likely smarting head in understanding at his dad. After listening to his father's explanation about how the world in that coffee shop worked, wise little Trent turned around and ran straight into the door *again*.

I think Trent did understand his dad. Being told not to run into a glass door is a practical piece of advice, and his dad was careful to explain it clearly. What Trent didn't get was that his father was actually recommending what was *best* for him (head included). Sometimes the fun of running makes the pain of colliding with a semi-invisible door unimportant.

How many of us have seen or participated in a loud conversation with a child in the ice-cream section of a grocery store? Or the candy aisle? If you look into the eyes of the kids arguing that filling the cart halfway full of ice cream is a good idea, you can see a lot of disbelief—disbelief that their parents could be so cruel or ignorant that they don't realize that "all ice cream all the time" is a fantastic idea. The stuff tastes *much* better than vegetables and it is easier to prepare, which can leave more time for TV or the Wii! This is truly a win-win!

But those kids are missing something. It isn't that the parents are against the children or want to throw their authority around. At least we hope not. No, when parents are parenting well and say no to their children, it is because they see something the children don't. This reasoning doesn't usually help, as children don't understand what they don't understand.

This continues into adulthood. How many of us have had to lead or be responsible for people who underestimate the complexity of our jobs and therefore think they could do them better? Consistently, books on management theory and practice say these are some of the hardest people to lead. Presumption is a powerful force, whether it is accurate or not.

Presumption is a powerful force, whether it is accurate or not.

What do little Trent and the kids in the grocery store have in common? They don't get what they don't get.

What About Us?

Could I pose a question? What if God is facing the same problem that we experience every time we walk down the candy aisle with little Johnny? What if he is responsible and caring, like most good parents? But what if he also has a level of awareness that we don't ourselves understand—that maybe even we aren't looking for? Maybe, when it comes to the issues of suffering and pain, it is we who don't get what we don't get.

Maybe, when it comes to the issues of suffering and pain, it is we who don't get what we don't get.

I am in no way trying to say that the confusion that arises when we or others experience deep pain is the same as a little kid wanting ice cream. I can imagine many kids enduring the nightmare of abusive parents or schoolyard bullying would give anything for lives where their greatest trial was not having ice cream until the veggies were finished. I am not saying these situations are equal in any way.

But what if the principle remains true?

Is it possible to be in relationship with someone and not fully appreciate the complexity of the responsibilities he or she must carry in that relationship? Further, if we do underestimate that complexity, can we arrive at inaccurate conclusions about how someone is handling his or her end of the bargain? And if we can do this with our bosses or our spouses, how much more so can we be open to making the same mistake with God?

He is infinitely more complex than we are and is responsible for more than we could ever begin to understand. Is it at least *possible* that as we witness his actions or inactions in the universe, we could be very wrong about why he does what he does?

Please hear me. My point isn't: *You have gotten it all wrong about God. He is a nice guy doing a great job.* If I tried to just sweep all our painful questions under the rug you wouldn't fall for it, and I struggle with some of those questions as well. But any good supervisor who is considering firing someone allows the employee to explain what has been going on. Let's allow God that.

Naked and Eating Fruit

Here is how the Scriptures would make the case for God's perspective on what is really going on here on earth.

It all started in the Garden of Eden. Adam and Eve had been created and had been given nearly free reign of the entire place. They had a sweet life and fulfilling work, were surrounded by all the food they could possibly want, and they got to walk around naked! Aside from some sunburn concerns, sounds pretty great to me.

Almost everything was at their disposal. And the *almost* really matters here. God, in what certainly seems to have been a face-to-face exchange with Adam, explained that one of the trees in the middle of the Garden should be left completely alone. God called it "the tree of the knowledge of good and evil." God was direct and succinct about the reasons they should steer clear: "If you eat its fruit, you are sure to die" (Genesis 2:17 NLT).

Eventually, Adam and Eve were tricked by a serpent to do

the very thing that God had warned them about. And the serpent's line was one that has run through every one of our heads ever since: *Someone is holding out on us.*

The serpent came up to them and spoke! Seems pretty far-fetched, and you do need to accept the presence of supernatural power (both for good and evil) in our world to buy it. Personally, I would have to say that if a snake comes up and says *anything* to me, I am out the metaphorical door! If my situation were like that of Adam and Eve, I would cut down a tree, build a door, and then run out of it. (I realize this is a ridiculous statement—not because I will never be in their situation, but because, as my wife says, "There is no way you could ever build a door that would be remotely useful.")

Let's remember, this whole thing was new to Adam and Eve, so they took the bait. They didn't know what should be speaking to them and what shouldn't. And it seems as if they were more concerned about missing out on something than they were with sticking to the clear instructions God had given them. The snake simply told them that God wanted to hold them back from experiencing everything they could. He didn't want them to have the really good stuff. God was stunting them.

And they fell for it.

They took a bite of whatever fruit there was, and, instantly, a chain of events was unleashed. (More on that later.)

I used to be very angry with God about that tree. Tempting them like that? It was only a matter of time before they wouldn't be able to restrain themselves. And then what? He blames *them*? How long did God expect they would make it before, to their ears, the "you can eat *everything* but that one tree" became "you can eat everything *but* that one tree"?

To Be Fair, Though . . .

God didn't say Adam and Eve should avoid any flowering shrubs over three feet tall (or I guess "a cubit" if we want to go old-school). He didn't say to also avoid any plant life that is green on every other Wednesday, and on the opposing Wednesdays to avoid the red stuff. None of the "leaves of three, let it be" nonsense. Whether we are okay with what he did or not, God was clear: "Stay away from that one tree, all the time."

I have come to appreciate the risk of that tree for God—and the necessity of that tree for us. Simply put, that tree made us real: it gave us choice. God wasn't looking to make some complicated hamsters that he could set up in a sweet cage. He created us for real relationship with him. Real relationship simply cannot exist if you cannot choose something else other than that relationship. We pity a woman whose husband or boyfriend keeps her locked in their house, monitors the few phone calls he allows her to have, and keeps even her family at arm's length. No one would call that love.

Had God not offered the tree and with it the opportunity to rebel against him, he would have been that guy. Love that isn't chosen is forced. In giving us that tree and making the warning very clear, he gave us choice, even the option to reject his guidance and companionship. He knew very well that decision would cost him dearly, but it was what was best for us.

Love that isn't chosen is forced.

But the results can still be confusing. God said if Adam and Eve ate that fruit they would die, but it looks as if they didn't. Was he faking? They didn't drop dead; the death that God was talking about was a spiritual one. They would become disconnected from God and even from each other. We can see that happened immediately. They became embarrassed that they were naked and tried to hide from God. Adam even tried to pin the whole thing on Eve! And we have been dealing with that reality ever since.

Maybe putting it another way would be useful.

Infection Unleashed

Imagine that it wasn't the eating of the fruit that created all the problems. Not the actual chewing and swallowing. It was the decision to bite into the fruit. Adam and Eve decided that God must not be as right as the serpent in front of them, so they passed the ol' fruit around. And imagine that when they bit into it, instead of its just being a regular piece of fruit, it released infectious spores everywhere. Those spores multiplied and spread rapidly over everything. We will call the infection *rebellion*.

This infection can and does reproduce without limit. It spreads everywhere and settles into everything to its deepest levels: the ground, the plant life, the animals, and even us. Some radioactive agents are much like this. They fly right through the skin and settle in our bloodstreams, or in certain organs. This one settles into the soul.

The infection of rebellion settles into the soul.

One of the symptoms of this infection is psychological. It hinders trust. It causes aggression. People start going after everyone else and work to protect and elevate themselves.

Once in our souls, this baby really gets going—like the cockroaches in my first apartment—constantly reproducing itself. And this is where the hopelessness of our situation really begins to take hold. The Bible makes the claim that none of us can free ourselves from this infection. Nothing works, not even the things we thought could.

This isn't just a minor point. What the Scriptures say is that even the planet was infected with rebellion. It is tough to imagine, but it seems God is saying the whole creation kind of went off the rails. We see an example of something "off the rails" and out of control, unfortunately, every day in cancer patients.

The Normal Becoming Abnormal

Something—we're not sure what—takes the very natural process of cell replication and causes it to go haywire. Cells start reproducing too quickly or begin producing the wrong things; in some cases, they simply don't die when they are supposed to. This is all because of something deep within the human body breaking down, a normal process becoming abnormal. Up to a few hundred years ago, things like cancer were thought to be caused by imbalances in our bodies' "humors"—four bodily fluids that in medieval times were thought to control a person's emotional and physical states. It took our looking much deeper to see the problem was that something unnatural had been triggered within the body's natural processes.

Just as our bodies' having cancer can sometimes only be discovered by symptoms that none of us would choose, a broken planet will have symptoms that were never the intention of its Creator.

A broken planet will have symptoms that were never the intention of its Creator.

Like most everyone, I know a number of people who have struggled against cancer. In my experience, most have won that fight. But cancer still remains one of the most feared diagnoses a patient can receive. It is also often one of the most complicated for physicians to treat. We probably all have stories of someone hearing the "There is simply nothing else we can do" speech. In our society, which so highly elevates personal choice and flexibility, this can be an especially stinging conclusion. We are immersed in a culture that allows us to do everything from ordering our burgers our way to setting up our own payment plans, to choosing the background for our Twitter home pages. So, beyond the clear implications of hearing that phrase pertaining to a battle with cancer, we are generally unaccustomed to hearing that our choices are severely limited.

And it is almost true.

The truth is that there is almost always another thing that can be done, almost always another step that can be taken against this medical horror. But the problem is that curing isn't just about eradicating the disease, is it? It is about eradicating the disease in such a way as to preserve the life of the patient, and even to allow for a certain level of life beyond cancer. In some cases the most effective and straightforward approach to removing the cancer would be to simply open the patient and take it out. Unfortunately, in many cases that would kill the patient. Other times, the patient would live but have no discernible quality of life. We hate these truths, and very wise and dedicated men and women work tirelessly to try to put them away; but for now, they are a reality that we must deal with.

God as Earth's Oncologist

May I pose a question? What if the same were true of God?

What if God hates the symptoms of this broken world as much as or more than we do? What if our suffering and pain burden him even more than they burden us? But what if there are issues that keep him from being able to eradicate our infection, our rebellion? What if his cure would actually kill us? Or what if it wouldn't kill us, but it would dehumanize us? What should God do then? What if God were less like a superhero not doing his job and more like the oncologist fighting the cancer of our rebellion every day? He would be personally watching the horrors it unleashes but know the treatment limits as well.

What if God hates the symptoms of this broken world as much as or more than we do?

Let's toss this idea around a bit.

Jesus deals with this issue in the Gospel of Matthew, the first book in the New Testament and an eyewitness account from one of Jesus' followers and good friends. He relates a story Jesus told that reveals how God is limited in doing everything he might like to do by the implications of those actions:

> The Kingdom of Heaven is like a farmer who planted good seed in his field. But that night as the workers slept, his enemy came and planted weeds among the wheat, then

slipped away. When the crop began to grow and produce grain, the weeds also grew. The farmer's workers went to him and said, "Sir, the field where you planted that good seed is full of weeds! Where did they come from?" "An enemy has done this!" the farmer exclaimed. "Should we pull out the weeds?" they asked. "No," he replied, "you'll uproot the wheat if you do. Let both grow together until the harvest. Then I will tell the harvesters to sort out the weeds, tie them into bundles, and burn them, and to put the wheat in the barn." (Matthew 13:24–30 NLT)

This scenario was meaningful to the people hearing it, many of whom relied on crops for their livelihood. It was bad news to find weeds growing among your wheat plants. You never wanted them there because they competed for resources your wheat needed, and in some cases they would choke out the much more delicate wheat plants. But as bad as it was, your acting in the most clear-cut way would exact terrible damage. Just pulling out what you didn't want was too damaging an option. You can just imagine those listening nodding their heads in agreement when Jesus said, "You will hurt the wheat if you do."

His point was very clear. If God did what we think he should and just removed all evil, it would exact a toll on us that we have no understanding of. See it? We are the wheat—and apparently we are the kids in the ice-cream aisle. God holds off doing what he would most want to, not for himself, but for us.

Can We at Least Have Less Evil?

But if we are honest, that only pushes the question back a step.

Even if we agree it is best for God to wait to ultimately deal with the evil infection in our world, our concerns about his management style deal directly with the amount of suffering that innocent victims must endure. Sure, maybe everything bad cannot be stopped just yet, but still, too much gets through. So, let's tighten that filter up a bit. Perhaps we will discover a cure.

If we were going to start picking things in our world that we would like to put an end to, devastating disasters would be a great place to start. No one would argue against the eradication of those. As storm fronts become supercells and start to create the noticeable spin that allows them to strengthen and create tornadoes, God could simply stop them. A cold or warm front at the right moment from the right direction means no homes destroyed, no vehicles tossed as if they were toys. No one has to die.

Eradicating ethnic cleansing and racist hatred would be agreed upon as well. Childhood hunger, millions of people being killed by malaria-bearing mosquitoes, human slavery and trafficking: again, no arguments. How great it would be to be able to make that list: "Horrors That Will Never Happen Again." God steps in and simply stops evil.

The big problem for the person who makes that list really isn't where you start, but where you stop. In a world where pain is constrained, what pain is allowable? Any? None? This really starts to get tricky. The cancer can be removed, but what kind of life will be left afterward?

The big problem for the person who makes that list really isn't where you start, but where you stop.

The Purpose of Pain

We cannot deny that some pain is useful. If we never noticed that we'd stepped on a piece of glass but instead continued to walk on that foot and didn't clean out and protect the wound—an infection could take the entire leg, even our life. That is and has always been the danger of most forms of leprosy. The disease doesn't kill off human tissue, as we once thought. It just deadens the nerve endings so that the victims cannot tell when they have injured themselves. They walk on sprained ankles until the swelling is too significant and permanent damage occurs.

This past summer, I inadvertently created a yellow jacket preserve in my yard. I discovered it one afternoon as I ran my lawn mower over their hole in the ground. That day I was stung ten to fifteen times. The next week, after thinking I had killed them all, they let me know they were just fine. I was stung fifteen to twenty more times. Most of these stings were on my feet (it takes a truly wise man to mow his grass in flip-flops a week after finding a hive of stinging insects in it). By the time a couple of days had passed, one of my feet was so swollen that the sting sites were evident holes on the tops of my feet. My skin was so swollen, it was almost tearing. Sounds nice, eh?

As much as I hated that feeling, it kept me off my feet, which was what my feet needed to heal. Pain served its purpose.

But let's get back to serious issues—the end of our list. What about intentional pain we cause or feel as a result of someone else's actions? Does God just take over our bodies to keep us from harming someone in anger? What would that make us if he did? It would be the equivalent of his placing us in the Garden, telling us about the tree, but levitating it just out of our reach—just in case we should mess up and reach for it. As nice as that sounds, we would no longer be free at that point. Our freedom requires our being able to hurt and to be hurt. Our freedom to make any decision at all seems to require our being able to make terrible ones too.

Our freedom to make any decision at all seems to require our being able to make terrible ones too.

Even if we could just eliminate intentional harm, how many of us have been hurt unintentionally? A breakup, a word said by someone in anger, a simple mistake. How about those times when we believed that we were wronged, only to later find out that wasn't the case? An inaccurately perceived wrong can hurt as badly as an actual one.

Should God take over at those points as well? Should he prohibit the breakup that we desperately did not want to happen? Where would that put the one who needs it to end? Does that person's pain not matter because our pain matters more?

Or what about the pain that causes us to make a decision

that works for our good? We decide we won't take bullying any-more from a cruel boss, so we finally break out of our comfort zone and go back to school or change jobs. What about all the powerful contributions of normal people in the world that started with the simple thought *I will never allow that to happen again*? What, if any, pain do we consider allowable? What do we do with the numbness that must take hold if pain isn't allowed? Would we ever grow tired of being pleasant robots?

We all agree that life without cyclones, mass shootings, and the abuse of innocent people is something we should strive for, but finalizing that list is where the problems lie.

A Tricky Spot

This puts God and us in a tricky spot. We desperately would like freedom from the infection of rebellion and its side effects. We understandably ask God for reprieve again and again. If he is right, then he looks much like the physician who wants more than anything to be able to heal us right now. But he knows, much more clearly than we do, that to eradicate the infection the way we prefer would either doom us to merely perpetuating the infection or guarantee the deaths of our souls.

For now it would seem that God has chosen a much more per-sonally painful path: no easy answers and no quick removal of all suffering. But no avoiding it for him either. Perhaps this is the clearest way he resembles an oncologist. As painful as our experi-ence with the cancer of our souls is, at some point it ends and we are able to move on. Not so for God. Just as the oncologist faces cancer in the lives of different people every day, God faces our pain constantly as well. The reality is that the God who created the universe is suffering right here with us. Right now.

The infection cost him the life of his Son.

The reality is that the God who created the universe is suffering right here with us. Right now.

Maybe he isn't turning his back on anything or anyone. Maybe he isn't a sullen superhero turning a deaf ear to our cries for help. Maybe he just sees the complexity that we miss. The Scriptures say that even though he cannot remove the horror of sin right now, that when the time is right, he will. For now he walks with us through our lives. And his grief is as real as ours.

Questions for Reflection and Discussion

1. When you read the account of the mother who let her daughter die, what did you think about? Why?

2. What do you think about what Jesus says in Luke 6:43–45:

No good tree bears bad fruit, nor does a bad tree bear good fruit. Each tree is recognized by its own fruit. People do not pick figs from thornbushes, or grapes from briers. The good man brings good things out of the good stored up in his heart, and the evil man brings

evil things out of the evil stored up in his heart. For out
of the overflow of his heart his mouth speaks. (NIV)

Do you agree? How have you seen this play out in your life?

3. Is it fair to apply this same reasoning to God? What additional issues does this bring up for you? Are these issues primarily emotional or logical? Why would you describe them this way?

4. In the section called "We Don't Always Get What We Don't Get," I talk about how parents are responsible for using their larger knowledge pool in their parenting. I said good parents do this even when it is frustrating, confusing, or even angering to their children. Have you ever experienced that with God?

5. How do you view the account of Adam and Eve in the Garden with a forbidden tree and a serpent? Is it actual fact, poetic description, or complete fiction? What influences your view of this?

6. Do you see the necessity of God's providing a tree that is off-limits? Do you see the connection between our being able to reject God and his guidance and love for us and our being free-choosing humans? If we could not reject him, what would be the implications for our relationship with him?

7. Has your view of the role of pain changed as a result of seeing how it impacts and saddens God?

5

God Can Really Make It Difficult

My wife and i took a short anniversary getaway to a little town with a nice bed-and-breakfast. And we wanted to treat ourselves to a great dinner. As we were driving down the road we realized that in this case, *small town* meant *no good restaurants*. As we drove to the next small town, we used my phone to google restaurants in the area. We looked up menus online and if we found something we liked, we searched for it on the portable GPS module that we had purchased so I wouldn't constantly get lost when I travel. Once we had the address loaded, we simply followed the bright pink line that instantly appeared straight to the front door.

I love technology. I mean, I really love it. It's instant and accurate. The voice on my GPS has been researched and focus-grouped so that the manufacturers know it can be easily heard without being jarring or distracting. Amazing.

Even the opening screen that comes up when I turn the power on, which tells me not to use the device while I am driving, has been researched. That way, when I do use it while driving, I can access everything with maximum ease. Millions of dollars, years of study and research led to this product. I like it.

There is nothing wrong with wanting things to be optimized for you. And there is nothing wrong with liking things to work fast. The problem isn't inherent in speed or the lack thereof. The problem comes when we must have it all the time: when the benefits are discerned as needs rather than just great things.

I have learned the hard way, in working with large groups of people, that what starts out as a pleasant surprise can quickly become an expectation. And once it is a normal expectation, there isn't much distance between that and its becoming a need.

I heard about a guy on an airplane who got angry when the high-speed Internet went down! On the plane! The man telling the story noted, "How quickly the world owes him something he knew existed only ten seconds ago." You get me, don't you?

How many of us can realistically imagine going back to the pre–cell phone, pre-Internet world? How would I ever know that one of my friends is starting his day slowly because of a *Scrubs* marathon were it not for Facebook, or would I have seen Awkward Family Photos were it not for Twitter? Even if at times we imagine how great a simpler life would be, realistically we have adjusted our lives to the point that those technologies play a key role. Our blessings have a way of becoming our necessities.

> **Our blessings have a way of becoming our necessities.**

Parental Evolution

Here is another way things strike us now. Today, many feel that a child-centric parenting style will best set their children up for success later in life. This style is predicated on the idea that opportunities for development in young children lead to greater long-term life success. The more you can give them, the better equipped for life they will be. Kids need music lessons by age three, language classes by five. Assuring later readiness for prep school can be in full swing by second or third grade. As a result, kids eleven through sixteen are becoming a formidable buying block as parents seemingly spare no expense in meeting the needs or desires of their little darlings. I know something about this, because three members of that formidable buying block are my little darlings.

Even universities are, as a result, dealing with a concept referred to as "helicopter parents." These are just what they sound like: parents hovering around where their children attend college, discussing students' grades with their professors, intervening in housing issues. There are even reports of parents accompanying their college graduates on their job interviews. Parents get hotel rooms for days after helping their children get things moved in and situated in their rooms. (Who knew how cruel my parents were for helping me to unload my stuff and then leaving me to set up my room and my new life?)

But, in all fairness, the things coming into those dorm rooms are quite a bit more involved as well. Once I helped a man unload a massive amount of furnishings for his daughter's freshman dorm room. Now realize, if they had stacked everything up to the ceiling, all the stuff they brought wasn't going to make it into that room. But the most striking thing was that after I helped carry up a forty-inch plasma TV, the father asked me who he would need to talk to about digging into the cinderblock wall so that the monitor could be flush mounted. And today, eighteen-year-olds driving Hummers to and from classes are much more frequent than they ever were when I was in college.

For many parents, this is how it is done. You do everything you can to bless those you love. You want that love to be easily noticed. And you would like that same courtesy in return. Immediacy becomes important for us; it is the language we most prefer to speak. But after a while, immediacy becomes a need itself. Waiting for what we want in life is more and more foreign. It feels cruel to withhold things from those we deeply care for.

We must realize this is a sociological phenomenon that combines a number of factors fairly specific to our culture. Our expectation of ease and accommodation hasn't been around forever, nor will it last forever—but it can feel timeless to us. Simply put, while our parents or grandparents were much more likely to delay gratification, we aren't. Our grandparents had no choice but to realize that life would not adjust to them, or if it did, only minimally. Our emerging generations are different. We are accustomed to surround sound, self-leveling color palettes, almost seamless wireless signals, no cords, and no fuss. As in the case of my portable GPS, we like our bright pink lines that lead us straight to our destinations.

So the conditions we were raised in and the conditions we live in now lead us to draw conclusions about what we can and should expect. Our environment adjusts our expectations. And those expectations can extend to God. This can make his way of developing his relationship with us very frustrating.

Everything Was Going So Well . . .

I was talking with a young woman who had been "in the zone" with God. As she put it, "God and I were on a roll! It got to where, if I asked him to do something for me, he would. I would just pray it out and then know that God would get right on it for me." She talked about God doing wild stuff all around her, filling her vision with the reality of his attentiveness to her. There was simply no real way to question it.

Have you been there? I have. Things just seem to be in sync between you and God. Even tough steps are easier to take because you are seeing such strong returns on your faith. Everything is working. After a while, you start trying to run the math, don't you? You know, kind of start looking for what the formula is. *Is it my new commitment to this Bible study? That I am stepping up into leadership? My service around my neighborhood? Is God doing this to show that he is pleased with my increased financial giving?*

The reason this woman was speaking to me was that God had started disappointing her. Her formula seemed to be breaking down. It seemed that just as often as he had granted her requests before, he now seemed to be turning a deaf ear. And she was really struggling.

Just as often as he had granted her requests before, he now seemed to be turning a deaf ear.

I really don't think this woman was trying to treat God like her own spiritual ATM, just punching in some numbers to get something back. She wasn't asking for things only for herself; in fact, those were the minority of what she asked God for. She was lifting up the legitimate needs of others around her.

The scary thing was that she was being very normal. Decidedly *unweird*. That's what reeks. If we could find some gross, horrific thing she was doing, some major mistake in how she was praying, some huge weak spot, then maybe God's seeming indifference would make sense. We could say, "Well, of course God cannot do that! Look at what is going on!" But there wasn't any great flaw. It just seemed as though God had started to say no to her. And if he did that with her, then we have to realize we will experience it too.

I remember one of the times when God said no to me.

Where Are You, God?

I had decided that God wanted me to be a pastor, the leader in a church. I was working on staff with the church that I copastor now. Tracy and I had felt this was the place to come, but nothing was working out. Tracy was miserable and every time I tried to step into a new leadership position, it seemed I got shut down.

People around me were flourishing. Everything seemed easier for them. It looked as if I was just getting left behind in life. Even our marriage seemed to be crumbling, so we sought counseling.

The counselor challenged me to see my wife's frustration as a means God could use to guide us. He challenged me to make a deal: If Tracy didn't feel as if she could handle being in what was at the time a very small, almost exclusively college student church, in six months we would find another one. I would admit that God wasn't actually calling us there, and we would move on.

I was really nervous about this; at the time, Tracy wasn't feeling superclose to God. What if she just wasn't listening to him? What if she wasn't giving our new church a fair shake? We had left a lot for this specific opportunity. What if we had to leave and go through all this again somewhere else? I remember God confirming with me that I should take the counselor's challenge, and then I remember God going silent.

I distinctly remember, time after time, going to God in my frustration. Maybe, somehow, he hadn't realized what was happening. This was my career! Tracy and I had left behind jobs and a plan for a PhD so we could come here and do this! I didn't know what made me more nervous: the idea that God had in fact not been paying attention to my life and this massive failure seemed to be coming, or the idea that he had—that God knew what was going on and wasn't doing everything at his disposal to stop it. It was as if he just suddenly left the table, dropped the phone, whatever—he just stopped talking to me.

I would like to say that my first response was to cross my hands and bow my head and say, "Well, Father, you must be up to something here. Speak when you are ready, and I will just focus on pursuing you in the meantime." Nope.

At first I got nervous. Then I got angry.

I remember trying to backtrack and figure out where I had done the wrong thing. Like hitting the Seek button on your car's stereo by mistake during a song you really like—you try to go back and find where you were. If you could just go back, the music you wanted would pick up again and everything would be fine.

But this was different. It wasn't that simple. It doesn't take much silence from God or confusion about that silence to make me feel very alone, and God and I hung out in that place for a long time.

I remember thinking, *Where are you, God?* I just needed to know a couple of things. And his choice of silence couldn't have come at a worse time.

So I have been there too. I know what it is like to really doubt the goodness of God, and I have watched many friends go through difficulties I would never wish on anyone. With our ministry so close to a university setting, I have intelligent cynics around me constantly. I have good friends who struggle as much with doubting the love of God as alcoholics struggle with the idea that life can be full and enjoyable without a drink.

I have friends who struggle as much with doubting the love of God as alcoholics struggle with the idea that life can be full and enjoyable without a drink.

Yesterday, one of my close friends, who is presently going through a more difficult struggle than I have ever faced, told me he feels trapped. He is too convinced of the reality of God to walk away from him, but he is getting angrier and angrier that God won't step into his pain in a more palpable way. It isn't that my friend wants every tough part of his life zapped magically away; he just wants to hear God speak in his struggle. And he isn't. And my friend is getting angrier.

Have you ever been in that place?

What Possible Reason Could There Be?

I mentioned in the introduction that I have a bad shoulder. After putting off surgery for years I bit the bullet and had my shoulder repaired, and now I am in the seemingly never-ending process of physical therapy. My physical therapists are great but make me do the most obscure exercises. I have gone to the gym and lifted weights for years, but these exercises are completely different. It seems that in my lifting, I have overemphasized certain muscles and virtually ignored others. So, part of my job is to balance things out a bit, which I must say I really do not enjoy.

I like doing what I have done. I like exercises I am comfortable with. They take less time and seem to have worked well enough. At least I thought that until a doctor really looked at my shoulder. It wasn't until a trained surgeon examined me that we saw my imbalance. I likely never would have caught it on my own.

That tendency toward imbalance doesn't live just in the realm of the gym and the deltoids. God faces that challenge with us all the time.

Once things have gone pretty well for enough time, we presume that is likely the best way for things to go *all* the time. We all have routines, procedures in our relationships with God, the way I had routines in the gym. Typically, if we are honest, many of us would find that if our relationships with God were carefully dissected, speed and clarity in our relationships with him would be high on our list of what we value.

That makes sense, doesn't it? If we are trying to understand God's opinion on an issue, especially one that is very important or carries a lot of weight, we can feel paralyzed if that opinion isn't given. Many times we feel as if we are waiting in good faith. We honestly want to know what God would say. Other times our distress is so significant we feel we *need* to hear from him.

C. S. Lewis, one of the greatest thinkers about God in the

last century, and someone who truly loved and desired to follow Jesus Christ, put it this way after losing his wife to cancer:

> When you are happy, so happy that you have no sense of needing Him, so happy that you are tempted to feel His claims upon you as an interruption, if you remember yourself and turn to Him with gratitude and praise, you will be—or so it feels—welcomed with open arms. But go to Him when your need is desperate, when all other help is vain, and what do you find? A door slammed in your face, and a sound of bolting and double bolting on the inside. After that, silence. You may as well turn away. The longer you wait, the more emphatic the silence will become.... What can this mean? Why is He so present a commander in our time of prosperity and so very absent a help in time of trouble?[1]

Knowing that Lewis eventually felt God's deep and close presence again provides only some solace. The questions remain: Why would he be silent when we need him to speak? Why not be direct, clear, and loud?

Why would he be silent when we need him to speak?

Even when things are exciting, we still value clarity and predictability. When I was starting to date my wife, I wanted to be as clear with her as I could be about how I felt...once I figured out exactly how I felt. I wasn't looking for intrigue, as I know many do. I wanted clarity. Was I feeling more for her than she was for me? Was I bugging her—was she bugging me? Where was this thing going? Why didn't she call me today? Why does she call me so much?

I love excitement as much as anyone. But in those most important areas of our lives, most of us would rather have clarity.

I started out in my relationship with God very similarly. I wanted to understand him; I wanted to "get" him. Sure, sometimes my motives weren't as good as I would have liked them to be. I was trying to get him to fit in my box, to be predictable so I could feel I was more in charge of my life than I actually was. I was never beyond just wanting to be right. But much of the time, probably like you, I thought my motives were, overall, pretty good.

I still want God to make sense to me. I want to be able to trust him more. I believe him when he tells me through Peter, the apprentice of Jesus, that my trust in him is more precious than my stuff. That my ability to trust him is more important to where my life is going than any possession I can get. That the value of my life with God is not tied to how much he gives me.

It is hard to grasp. But I have come to learn over the years that in those times, God is always up to something.

I still want God to make sense to me.

He Waited, Then He Whispered

I think that is the reason my physical therapists have told me to stop doing overhead presses and to start swishing my hand around in a five-gallon bucket of dry rice. And I suspect it is the same reason that God specifically came to Elijah in the most unlikely way. Elijah was a prophet in the Old Testament. Think of prophets as ancient performance artists. God would tell them something and they would communicate it to the people God intended it to go to. Here is one account of Elijah's receiving communication from God:

> [Elijah] went into a cave and spent the night. And the word of the LORD came to him: "What are you doing here, Elijah?" He replied [to God], "I have been very zealous for the LORD God Almighty. The Israelites have rejected your covenant, broken down your altars, and put your prophets to death with the sword. I am the only one left, and now they are trying to kill me too." The LORD said, "Go out and stand on the mountain in the presence of the LORD, for the LORD is about to pass by." Then a great and powerful wind tore the mountains apart and shattered the rocks before the LORD, but the LORD was not in the wind. After the wind there was an earthquake, but the LORD was not in the earthquake. After the earthquake came a fire, but the LORD was not in the fire. And after the fire came a gentle whisper. When Elijah heard it, he pulled his cloak over his face and went out and stood at the mouth of the

cave. Then a voice said to him, "What are you doing here,
Elijah?" (1 Kings 19:9–13 NIV)

If you know the account of Elijah and what had been happening over the past couple of chapters of 1 Kings, you know
God had done some pretty wild stuff. Elijah was on a roll! A
showdown of sorts on top of Mount Carmel, where Elijah had
to show massive courage in following what God had told him to
do. Then, after an amazing encounter between Elijah and several hundred demonic priests, the prophet became racked with
panic. He fell from the heights of faith to the depths of fear.

God led him to a cave and met with him there—but in the
strangest way. God first brought these massive signs: an earthquake and a fire. Both were common ways God had spoken to
the Israelites in the past, and he had just shown up as a blazing
fire in Elijah's showdown with the demonic priests.

But God points out that he wasn't in those signs this time.
And God made Elijah wait through those and listen very carefully for a gentle whisper.

Culturally, that wasn't how the Israelites expected God to be.
He had been a pillar of fire and smoke; he had shaken Mount
Zion; he had pushed back water to make a path of dry land.
These are not low-key methods of presenting yourself to people.
But here, God did something very different.

He went against Elijah's expectations. God wanted to give
Elijah, and through Elijah give all the people of Israel, a greater
sense of how he could present himself and make himself known.
He wanted to give them a broader sense of who he was. And

Elijah, like the rest of us, wouldn't catch the lesson as viscerally had God sent him a memo. Nope, God knew this lesson needed to be given through experience to be truly grasped. Maybe not as straightforward, maybe more time-consuming, but hey, God wanted him to get it. So instead of blasting onto the scene, he waited, and then he whispered.

He was quieter because he was doing something larger. Remember that Elijah was honestly feeling he had failed God or perhaps that God had failed him. He was very afraid for his life. If we were in God's shoes, we would likely say this was the *perfect* time to speak loudly, powerfully.

Predictably.

He was quieter because he was doing something larger.

Again, God seemed to feel differently.

You might say, "At least God spoke to Elijah! I would be happy with a whisper right about now." I also have felt that many times. But to say that would miss the point. God wasn't just being quiet, he was being unexpected. He was showing Elijah, even in the depths of his fear, that Elijah could never truly predict how God would speak to him. And remember, God guided the writers of the Scriptures to record these events for us. His intention was that we would trust the Bible and know that he would be the same with us as with Elijah.

**God wasn't just being quiet, he was being
unexpected.**

But God's unpredictability makes it hard to learn to trust
him.

What Might That Look Like Now?

Let's agree that much of what God was doing with Elijah that
day was showing him that cultural expectations do not limit
God. What does that mean for us?

One thing it can mean is that we should expect God to
thwart our culture's attempts to box him up. At some point in
our relationships with God, our cultural love affair with speed
and clarity will need to be dealt with.

**We should expect God to thwart our culture's
attempts to box him up.**

What clarity and speed have done for us is *not* what
was expected in the 1950s, when the staffs behind maga-
zines like *Popular Mechanics* predicted we would continue to
advance technologically. They envisioned our having personal robots by now; that we would be wearing unitards and
working a solid twenty-hour workweek. We would have more

time to be together. Living "la vida loca," as Ricky Martin would say.

In imagining such things, they were wrong about more than the unitard, weren't they? We now work *more hours* than people did in the fifties, and our families are actually together *less*. Technology hasn't brought us together; it has tended to separate us.

Let me ask you a question: What if living as individuals isn't wrong, but we have overrelied on our individualism? What if we aren't culturally completely wrong, just unbalanced, as I was in my workout regimen? And what if God saw that as a problem? What would he do?

What if God deeply values our relating to him in community as well? What if he never intended for us to get everything we need from him one-on-one? What would he do if our expectation was for him to always get back to us personally and quickly, much as those in Elijah's day always expected him to come with earthquakes, thunder, and fire?

It seems as though he would do the thing we least expect so that we would know he is there too. He would initially frustrate us so we could see he is larger than we ever thought. And to be fair, he hasn't been cryptic about this. Listen to what he led the author of Hebrews to write: "Encourage one another daily, as long as it is called Today, so that none of you may be hardened by sin's deceitfulness" (3:13 NIV). By checking out the context of this verse, you'll see that encouraging one another daily would provide a sense of protection. God would meaningfully speak through those around you in community—and we would mutually guide one another. Encouragement was intended for times of distress and difficulty.

Forget about the greeting-card version of encouragement we toss around now. Forget about the pictures of the kittens and puppies with little pithy sayings under them. The word that is translated for us as "encouragement" has little to do with that image. The word *encourage* was intended to mean that we would make one another more courageous...stronger. We would meaningfully guide each other through this life. The passage suggests that the community of people on a journey following Christ could be a meaningful help to one another in especially those times.

He didn't just drop us into some existential cubicle with an *Encyclopedia of God* for our reference and ease. And yet that is precisely what so many followers of Jesus are indirectly asking for. Rather, God is constantly calling us out of our cubicles and into deep and meaningful community with one another. It isn't just another way to experience his love; it is a far better way to do so. And so there are times when God seems to be willing to simply be silent. To not speak as we might culturally expect him to, so that we can attune our ears and eyes to searching more deeply for him.

God is constantly calling us out of our cubicles and into deep and meaningful community with one another.

He never acts in some arrogant and mean-spirited manner, but rather as a means of keeping us balanced. He doesn't seem opposed to speaking directly to us on a moment's notice—or not doing so. He seems to constantly be looking for what will guide us into a deeper and richer experience of himself and his creation.

In his phenomenal book *The Divine Conspiracy*, Dallas Willard says this:

> Jesus shows his apprentices how to live in the light of the fact that they will never stop living.... According to the wisdom of Jesus, then, every event takes on a different reality and meaning, depending on whether it is seen only in the context of the visible or also in the context of God's full world, where we all as a matter of fact live.[2]

As we are able to grasp more fully the lives Jesus is calling us to live, we will become more and more intrigued by the challenges we face. Even our difficulties, while still stinging, are filled with a meaning that only God is able to grant them. Nothing gets easier. It just gets more meaningful.

Nothing gets easier.
It just gets more meaningful.

Video Games and God

My oldest son loves video games. And he has a remarkable ability to navigate them. He can go through these incredibly intricate epic worlds and remember, not just where to go in them, but what is hidden in them that he will need later. I clearly remember one instance when our neighbor, a father of two, was asking Noah how to navigate one of those worlds and how Noah immediately guided him through it from memory, all while jumping on our trampoline.

Meanwhile, I struggle to get past the beginner level in *Guitar Hero*.

A little over a year ago, Noah discovered something amazing: cheats. Cheats are codes you can find online and then input into the game that help you to never die, to have unlimited power, to find hidden entrances, and so on. What Noah found was that, at first anyway, the game was instantly more fun. He was able to predict the outcomes of his attempts, and he was unhurt by all but the most significant beatings. But those beatings were few and far between as he was able to utilize his premium firepower to overcome most foes.

He also discovered something else. The predictability he gained and the power he was able to wield led to the game's being almost pointless. He could win very quickly, and there was little challenge to it. He found that he was just walking through the paces needed to move toward the inevitable win. The wins meant less and he found himself ultimately bored.

We can be a bit like Noah. Given the chance in life, we would like to have all the "cheats"—at least for a while. We almost certainly would go for them if given the chance. Cheats would sure come in handy when it seems as though our kids, our marriages, or our physical or emotional health is heading for the cliff. Who wouldn't want to just skip forward to see if the interview you are preparing for would result in a great job, or if the blind date you are subjecting yourself to will result in something meaningful—knowing all your effort, sacrifice, and risk will soon pay off? I would have given an awful lot when Tracy and I were going through our six-month period of deciding if we would stay where we were to know how that would eventually work out. The idea of going straight for the solution you are certain will work could be really great.

Please know that I am in no way saying that difficulties encountered in a video-game world are of the same importance as those that our very real world can hurl at us. Certainly not. But our desires run in similar directions to the desires of someone wanting to win at a video game. What we very often want from God, what we can get angry that he doesn't provide, in essence, are the cheats.

Cheats, in their most basic form, offer predictability and insulation from pain and the consequences of the actions of others. They offer us control. They put things in our time frame. No more hours and hours spent in the search for the hidden doorway or in trying one move again and again. No more risking all that time and effort only to not have it work the way we need it to. Quicker, cheaper wins.

Our motives aren't bad, at least not most of the time. Probably we are a lot like the hearers of the Hebrews letter or Elijah. Not perfect, certainly, but not all bad either. And our desires for clarity and answers from God when we ask for them aren't all bad either. They make sense. But they remove the power of the moment when what we have so searched for is revealed.

Our desires just aren't balanced. God knows his silence can make life very difficult for us. He tells us multiple times throughout the Scriptures that he experiences our pain personally.

Otherwise he wouldn't have devised a plan to cure the infection of rebellion we suffer from that cost him the life of his own Son. No, he doesn't insulate us from as much confusion and suffering as we would like, but neither does he insulate himself.

He is aware of us intimately. But God sees that we tend to wall ourselves off and actually experience much less than what he is actually offering us. And he sees a beauty when we come together in community with one another that we often miss.

**God knows his silence can make life very difficult
for us.**

In the same way that God isn't being flippant or cruel, my physical therapists are not sadists—at least not completely. But they are willing to frustrate me and even cause me some pain if it is necessary in the long run. They see my shoulder strong and unhampered by the harm I have caused it. And they are moving me there.

May we all reap the benefits of having people around us who see what we cannot so that we won't stop when we must not. This is what God does with us in a world of pain. This is where trust is rooted.

We'll look at that next.

Questions for Reflection and Discussion

1. Do you like technology the way I do? If so, why?

2. Do you see how speed and clarity are expectations in our

culture? To what extent are you frustrated when you feel that something is either too slow or too confusing? How do you respond to being slowed down or inconvenienced in your day-to-day life?

3. Do you find yourself applying that thought process to your interactions with God—do you ever think God has chosen to be either unclear or slow to answer you? Reflecting back, can you determine any reason he might have had for doing that? How did you respond while you were experiencing his seeming silence?

4. Why would it have been natural for Elijah to assume that when God spoke it would be with great volume and power? Why do you think God valued being unexpected by Elijah?

5. Imagine Elijah were alive and the interaction recorded in 1 Kings 19 were occurring today. Now imagine that God wanted to communicate with Elijah in a way that would be considered unexpected based on what our cultural expectations of him are. How would he go about doing that?

6. Is it your expectation and understanding that when God speaks to you, it will always be on an individual basis? Do you value his guidance just as much when it comes through others as when it comes through the Scriptures?

7. If you are being honest, would you rather just have God give you the "cheats" to ensure you a happy, healthy, and prosperous life?

6

A Terrible Risk

Jim, noah would like to play baseball this season."

That was all it took.

When I say that I wasn't good at sports growing up, I mean it. I was the one most people didn't want on the team. On three separate occasions in elementary school, the time that you really start to see the differences between the coordinated kids and people like me, teachers had to break up arguments between captains of teams who couldn't decide who would have to take me. Three times. Once in ninth grade too.

I distinctly remember making faces and acting silly and trying to make jokes, but just wishing I could find a hole somewhere and crawl into it. Those PE classes were some of the longest in my life. The only good thing about them was that they ended.

Or so I thought.

Noah is similar to me. He's more coordinated than I was at that age, but he's still not able to perform at the level of some of the other boys his age. The first time he asked if he could play baseball I panicked. Have you ever had one of those moments when so many things are flying around in your head at once that nothing really seems to make sense?

We want our children to be involved in sports so they will be physically active and develop a sense of team play. That is important, right? But in the back of my mind, as soon as Noah mentioned baseball, I was right back there on the bench in the dugout, waiting until the game was out of reach for either our team or theirs for me to get a chance to get in. I remembered the sighs that the better players would make as I made my way to home plate. I remembered my coach telling those guys that we were a team and they needed to cheer for everybody on the team, including me. I remember getting nervous as the other team's catcher started with the normal home-plate chatter. Then my mind went to static. I would forget how to "just make contact with the ball." I would forget to "watch it all the way to the bat." I would forget everything.

The sad thing was that I was really fast, so if I could get on base, I could steal all the way around and even home. But if I wasn't walked, I almost never made it to first. That ball is already pretty small, and on the flight to home plate it seemed to almost disappear to my half-closed and squinty eyes. I can still remember the feel of Jackson Street's baseball field, the sound of the umpire's loud voice just behind me calling out "Strike three!" The catcher cheering, and my coach doing the "That's all right; we'll get 'em next time!" clap for me. You could tell by the looks on the faces of my team members that they didn't buy it, and I didn't either.

My panic for Noah mixed with a frantic prayer: "God, please let him be better at this than I was so that he doesn't have to feel what I felt—Wait a second; the goal shouldn't be that everything is easy for him—he needs to go through difficulty with us around so he can learn from it with our help and guidance—But God, that was so awful, can't you do this another way? This is not to say that I don't trust you, God; he is your son and you are a better guide of his life than I am—but wait a minute, do I really believe that? I mean, if I really believe that then I should be more willing to allow God to walk him through whatever he needs—What is this saying about my faith? Have I not been honest with myself and everybody else about the level of trust I have in God?" All this would burst around in my head and come out at one hundred miles per hour.

**God, that was so awful,
can't you do this another way?**

A lot of confused prayer came out of my lips and heart as the time drew closer to sign him up for a team.

A Storm Builds

Baseball for Noah started out very well, much better than it had for me. Things were looking good. Then about halfway through the season the wheels started coming off the cart. He had a couple of strikeouts in a row—frustrating, but normal for almost everyone. But the next game he struck out every time he went to the plate.

He didn't hit the ball again that season.

I remember the feelings; the nervous look on his face was the same one I remembered having. The eyes that were mostly closed instead of being wide open to watch the ball. The bat that shot out to where you were hoping the ball would be instead of making a smooth arc to where it was. Getting angry at yourself for swinging wide when you shouldn't, then while you were still angry watching a perfect strike come floating in right after it while your bat stayed on your shoulder. I remember all of it. And I was watching the storm build on his face.

One game, it just became too much. He finally broke down in anger and frustration and embarrassment, and his team saw him break. And he knew it.

I walked behind the dugout when it was time for him to take right field. He looked up and begged me not to make him go out there. He just wanted to go home. He was hot and tired and embarrassed and why couldn't we *just leave?* And I was right back at Jackson Street feeling the exact same feelings.

I was a buddy with his coach; I could have pulled him out. The coach would have understood; everyone would have. And in that moment, all I wanted to do was rescue him and get him out of there. I wanted to help him stop feeling the horrible stuff that I so very well remembered. And as I looked down at my son, his face red with the heat and frustration, I realized something.

I absolutely could not do it.

So many times as parents, we have to go with our gut. Scripture gives us some guidance, but God (not surprisingly) was wise enough to know that the approach to parenting would need to adjust to the times in which the parents and children were living. So Scripture handles parenting mostly from a principle standpoint, more of the way you approach things and less of what you do here, here, and here. So I pray a lot for a God-guided, faith-filled gut. And in that moment, I felt I heard from God clearly and specifically.

Noah needed to go out into the outfield with his team. And I had to tell him.

Putting Power Aside

In that moment, I had all the power in the world to control that situation. I could make it easier for Noah—even make it easier for myself. As much as I hated that part of my life, I would have traded with him in a second if I could have. But I couldn't. As embarrassed as he was, as frustrated and angry and disappointed and hot and ready to leave as he was, he needed to stay. There was much more going on in that moment than he had any idea about. And I was responsible for the fact that I knew what it was.

I knew I wouldn't be able to exercise the power in the situation that I had available to me. Noah had to learn the importance of keeping his commitments, of not giving in to fear and embarrassment, of trying as hard as he could even when those attempts didn't result in the outcomes he was looking for. He had to learn that even when you desperately don't want to take the field, if you have said you will, you do it. Most important, he needed to see that he could.

So, on that day, to use all the power I had available to me would have been selfish. It would have made us both feel better, but some lessons can only be learned with stinging eyes on the way to right field.

A *Little Bit of an Idea*

Out of nowhere, in that moment I got just the smallest sense of what it might be like to be God. That God might feel the way I felt that day behind that dugout, with someone I loved more than I could describe getting sadder and angrier at me and realizing he needed to continue to walk down the path that had caused him pain. To have the power to remove the struggle, but knowing the removal isn't in the best interest of the child, is a painful place to be. Making decisions based on a larger *right* is always tougher. But sometimes it is unavoidable.

Making decisions based on a larger *right* is always tougher. But sometimes it is unavoidable.

The point here is not whether I did the right thing in that moment or not. Neither is it just that it pains the heart of God to allow difficulty to get to us that he would rather, in a (literally) perfect world, restrain. The real issue here is the response from Noah. He didn't get what my goals were and if he did, he certainly was on the side of reaching them a different way. As I said before, he didn't understand what he didn't understand. From his vantage point, a loving father would behave differently. If *he* were a father, he would behave differently. It was a very straightforward issue from where he was sitting. We should go. We could handle the other stuff in other ways. But right now, in this moment, we should head home.

Again, we have to consider the ramifications of bailing out. We need to constantly remember that we can understand only parts of God. He has made himself knowable to us through the Scriptures and through the experiences people have had with him across time. We get to know God through truly giving ourselves to and appreciating his creation—not looking to use any part of it selfishly, but seeing every part of it as a divine signpost pointing us back to him.

But even then, we can get only part of him. We will never be able to understand the fullness of God's thoughts, concerns, and plans. At least not while we are living on a broken planet. The New Testament tells us now we see things the way they saw things in mirrors of the first century: not clearly. Today we can make mirrors that will reflect whatever we need them to—everything from images on Mars to seeing if those jeans really do make our butts look big. But back then, mirrors were made from hammered bronze or other metals. You could see yourself—but just hazily.

Maybe if God wanted to make this idea clear to us in our context he would say, "Now you see unclearly, the way you would if you set your display setting to 256 colors." We would get the gist of what the picture was about, but that's about it.

This being said, if we don't get him, then we also don't get the larger picture that he is moving us toward. Just as surely as Noah didn't see what I was up to that day in the field, we don't get what God is up to on a daily basis. Just as surely as Noah's lack of understanding made him angry with me, our lack of understanding of what God is fully up to can make us angry with him. And just as surely as I still needed to respond to the larger picture that I knew brought risk of Noah's anger, God must do the same. And the risk is large.

Our lack of understanding of what God is fully up to can make us angry with him.

Our Infectious Situation

Remember how I described the Garden of Eden? Let's take it from a different angle this time. We observe Eve wandering over to the tree and taking a bite, then giving the fruit to Adam.

Scripture is very clear about what God had said to them: "You may freely eat the fruit of every tree in the garden—except the tree of the knowledge of good and evil. If you eat its fruit, you are sure to die" (Genesis 2:16–17 NLT).

When Adam and Eve took their bites from the fruit of the forbidden tree, an infection was released onto the planet that had up to that point been bound inside the fruit. When they broke the skin, the infection was released.

We have been living in the legacy and reality of that infection ever since. Our souls are infected at birth and our souls continue to spew the stuff. Frank Peretti says that is the reason you never have to sit down with your toddlers and teach them to be selfish. "Now, now, little Johnny. There you go being nice again, sharing those toys. Go on, keep it for yourself!" The infection covers us like a film. And we all have been infected by it for so long that we don't even notice anymore. The side effects continue, but they, as well, go unnoticed. Things have been operating in a broken manner for so long that it stops feeling broken at some point.

We rage against one another; we war; we cheat. And either we battle our nature our entire lives or we come to a point where we decide it is actually good and right to be the way we are. Most significantly, we remain separated from God.

This is not God's desire. Intrinsic to the infection is the rejection of his leadership, his guidance, even his company. We have essentially pushed him off the dance floor he built himself and us and said that we could take care of ourselves, thank you very much. And he has honored that.

At great personal risk.

The Father Who Did It All Wrong

One of the most famous stories Jesus told is the parable of the two sons:

> There was a man who had two sons. The younger one said to his father, "Father, give me my share of the estate." So he divided his property between them.
>
> Not long after that, the younger son got together all he had, set off for a distant country and there squandered his wealth in wild living. After he had spent everything, there was a severe famine in that whole country, and he began to be in need. So he went and hired himself out to a citizen of that country, who sent him to his fields to feed pigs. He longed to fill his stomach with the pods that the pigs were eating, but no one gave him anything.
>
> When he came to his senses, he said, "How many of my father's hired men have food to spare, and here I am starving to death! I will set out and go back to my father and say to him: 'Father, I have sinned against heaven and against you. I am no longer worthy to be called your son; make me like one of your hired men.'" So he got up and went to his father.
>
> But while he was still a long way off, his father saw him and was filled with compassion for him; he ran to his son, threw his arms around him and kissed him.
>
> The son said to him, "Father, I have sinned against

heaven and against you. I am no longer worthy to be called your son."

But the father said to his servants, "Quick! Bring the best robe and put it on him. Put a ring on his finger and sandals on his feet. Bring the fattened calf and kill it. Let's have a feast and celebrate. For this son of mine was dead and is alive again; he was lost and is found." So they began to celebrate.

Meanwhile, the older son was in the field. When he came near the house, he heard music and dancing. So he called one of the servants and asked him what was going on. "Your brother has come," he replied, "and your father has killed the fattened calf because he has him back safe and sound."

The older brother became angry and refused to go in. So his father went out and pleaded with him. But he answered his father, "Look! All these years I've been slaving for you and never disobeyed your orders. Yet you never gave me even a young goat so I could celebrate with my friends. But when this son of yours who has squandered your property with prostitutes comes home, you kill the fattened calf for him!"

"My son," the father said, "you are always with me, and everything I have is yours. But we had to celebrate and be glad, because this brother of yours was dead and is alive again; he was lost and is found." (Luke 15:11–32 NIV)

You just cannot get away from the fact that this parable is all wrong. In the Middle Eastern culture of Jesus' day, it would have been wrong for the dad to run out to the son who had disgraced him so. Older men in that culture simply didn't run. After all, the son, who symbolizes us in this story, had given his father the metaphorical finger. He had asked for his inheritance—right now! It was the same thing as saying, "I wish you were dead!" Talk about entitled and disrespectful.

We see how the story goes, the son spending his inheritance on parties and sex, finally running out of money. In a defining note, Jesus has the young man working with pigs, a very unclean animal to Jews. Jesus was clearly trying to make the son as rebellious and offensive as possible. He had turned his back on his family (which was a *much* larger insult then than it is now), rejected his people's traditions, and sought endless pleasure. The son even had to be very poor for quite a while before he considered going back.

But the reason the story seems wrong is the risk the father took. He clearly missed his son; you can tell by the way he was watching for him to return and how he ran to him when the boy finally appeared. But the father left *returning* in the hands of the son. He didn't go after him and drag him back, didn't have some muscle-bound servants go find him. He waited.

He risked.

He risked the son's never coming back, so that if the son did return, it would be because he chose to. The father would not force the son to be in relationship with him.

That is precisely the way God is with us. He doesn't use the power at his disposal any more than the father in the parable used his. Like the father in the parable, God has been wronged by us, and deeply so, but also like the father in the parable, he watches desperately for us to come back to him. He must restrain himself for us, and he does so.

So, when we reject him and choose to go our own way, even when we start to replace him with gods that we have contracted or imagined into existence, he sorrowfully allows it. He gives us our distance. He watches us, loves us, but keeps his distance.

He watches us, loves us, but keeps his distance.

Mostly.

From the moment God had to close down the Garden of Eden and release Adam and Eve into the world they had inextricably broken (they were already aware they had made a terrible decision), he started showing people how they could reconnect with him.

He began this with a series of inoculations.

An Act of Faith

In my younger years I was subjected to the same slurry of disease-fighting shots that everyone else was. Every few years I would have to get in the car, go with my mom to Dr. Powell's office, and allow her to stick a needle in me to protect me. Then, a few years later, we would do the same thing again (same mom, same doctor; the only thing that changed was my growing embarrassment with letting her give me the shot in my butt). Those inoculations essentially gave me protection from certain diseases for a certain amount of time. That protection wouldn't last forever, hence the need to go back and flash the cheeks to the doctor.

If we consider what is going on, this whole transaction seems a bit strange. You go somewhere and pay money so you can expose a private part of yourself to someone you barely know. Then they stick a very sharp object through your skin and inject a weakened form of the very disease you are attempting to avoid. You do this because you have been led to believe by those you trust that this very process will actually *reduce* the likelihood you will get sick.

If you will allow me the use of a bit of the lingo of my industry, that is an act of faith and trust.

Sure, shots are a bit different. You could research their effectiveness, but how many of us personally have? Faith-based "inoculations" have been around a long time. In the time predating the resurrection of Jesus, this inoculation routine was called *the sacrificial system*. When you read the Pentateuch (the first five books of the Bible), what you see, among other things, is God establishing a means by which his people could show their trust in him. The biblical books that people say are the most boring are Leviticus, Numbers, and Deuteronomy, where the sacrificial system is most described. God takes his people through some detailed instruction about how they can live and demonstrate to others that God was who he said he was and that they chose living with his presence. In their words, they were demonstrating their faith in the God of their patriarchs, Abraham, Isaac, and Jacob.

Faith-based "inoculations" have been around a long time.

You see in those books God showing the Israelites how to live in a way that was noticeably different from the way people around them lived. This was to develop in the Jews a strong sense of identity, to attract attention from the people living around them (whom God just as desperately loved), and to guide those people away from the prevailing cultural false-god and idol worship systems that had already spread as a result of the sin infection.

God set up a spiritual, heart-level inoculation not all that different from the ones we take to fight off disease. God's system had all those component parts; they were just put in a different order. He provided a means for people to choose him and in that choosing, to receive a temporary inoculation of the soul against the infection of rebellion. Graciously he left out the needle-in-the-rear aspect.

In *this* case, the important part of the process was the trust that led to the involvement in his sacrificial system. When we are dealing in the realm of inoculation from disease, the trust issue just gets you in the door and keeps you in the outdated waiting room reading outdated copies of *Highlights* until your turn comes.

With the Jewish sacrificial system, the obedience shown in the sacrifice revealed that you really did trust God's process of being reconnected to him. These beliefs were very attractive to the Jews as well as other people, as they gelled most clearly with the infection that everyone was suffering from. The false-god and idol systems allowed people a way to feel a sense of control over their gods. Worshiping those gods let the worshipers numb the awareness everyone had and has that there is a true God and that something isn't right in the relationship. These systems weren't just unhelpful in that they didn't reconnect anyone with the true God; they produced harmful side effects as well.

In his wonderful book *Surprised by Hope*, N. T. Wright says it like this:

> When human beings give their heartfelt allegiance to and worship that which is not God, they progressively cease to reflect the image of God. One of the primary laws of human life is that you become like what you worship; what's more, you *reflect* what you worship, not only back to the object itself but also outward to the world around. Those who worship money increasingly define themselves in terms of it and increasingly treat other people as creditors, debtors, partners or customers rather than as human beings. Those who worship sex define themselves in terms of it (their preferences, their practices, their past histories) and increasingly treat other people as actual or potential sexual objects. Those who worship power define

themselves in terms of it and treat other people as either collaborators, competitors, or pawns. These and many other forms of idolatry combine in a thousand ways, all of them damaging to the image-bearing quality of the people concerned and of those whose lives they touch.[1]

So God gave the Jewish people a way to demonstrate that they were about something different. But again, it was very risky.

Then Heaven Lit Up

God wanted to help everyone see the reality of his presence and then to demonstrate that belief. The sacrifices and the often-times wild-sounding rules for life were all intended to allow a Jew to be immersed in life with God while being surrounded by those who didn't follow him.

As the Jews demonstrated a life lived God's way, especially as they participated in the required sacrifices, God was free to inoculate them from the infection. The sacrifices needed to be regularly repeated, just like my shots. This was the way of the world for several thousand years.

Then God went quiet. For four hundred years, he didn't speak to the people, priests, or high priests of Israel—not to anybody. For four hundred years, not a recorded word from heaven.

Then heaven lit up.

God came back to the planet he created. He came as God

the Son, Jesus of Nazareth. This Jesus was a unique human in that he wasn't infected with sin at birth as we all are. Don't get me wrong—he was human in that he was gestated in the womb of Mary of Nazareth. She was a real, historical woman and she had a real, historical baby. The difference was that the baby wasn't formed from a sexual interaction in which her egg was fertilized by a male sperm cell. In this case, God simply initiated the pregnancy in her womb. The Bible describes this process in very broad brushstrokes in the first chapter of Luke:

> Gabriel greeted her: "Good morning! You're beautiful with God's beauty, beautiful inside and out! God be with you." She was thoroughly shaken, wondering what was behind a greeting like that. But the angel assured her, "Mary, you have nothing to fear. God has a surprise for you: You will become pregnant and give birth to a son and call his name Jesus. He will be great, be called 'Son of the Highest.' The Lord God will give him the throne of his father David; he will rule Jacob's house forever—no end, ever, to his kingdom." Mary said to the angel, "But how? I've never slept with a man." The angel answered, "The Holy Spirit will come upon you, the power of the Highest hover over you; therefore, the child you bring to birth will be called Holy, Son of God. And did you know that your cousin Elizabeth conceived a son, old as she is? Everyone called her barren, and here she is six months' pregnant! Nothing, you see, is impossible with God." And Mary said, "Yes, I see it all now: I'm the Lord's maid,

ready to serve. Let it be with me just as you say." (Luke
1:28–38 MSG)

What we see here is a confused young woman, as anyone
would be, yet ready to follow the lead of God.

So Jesus is fully human and fully God at the same time. That
fact is completely impossible and illogical for us if we are relying
on human logic and wisdom. But if we factor in that the God
who created logic is able, at his discretion, to supersede that same
logic, then a superlogical or supernatural outcome makes sense.

Again, it's risky, allowing a young woman such a prominent
role in his plan for the planet and doing it in such a crazy way!
What if she was just too young to be up to handling the task?

Deciding What Is Real

Clearly, you have to buy into the supernatural's being real
to believe any of this account. To naysayers I would say that
if there is a God who started the whole creation, then he has
already shown the intelligence and power to do whatever he
feels is necessary at any point.

To me, not only is the supernatural possible, but providing
for our reconciliation in an astounding way also seems exactly
what a supernatural God would do. Like the father in the story
of the two sons, he would provide a way to be reunited, but he
would not make that reunion a requirement. He would need to,

by definition, make that reunion rejectable. But that wasn't the only issue he had to contend with in this part of his plan.

Providing for our reconciliation in an astounding way also seems exactly what a supernatural God would do.

Remember, there was an infection raging everywhere. Everyone had it, including young Mary. Jesus had to be human enough to be a meaningful antidote for us and yet he had to be infection-free so the antidote would be useful.

As a result of being God, Jesus wasn't infected, but as a human, he was subjected to the temptations and difficulties that the infection brings to all of us. He was mistreated and frustrated at times. He saw things that made him angry, and ultimately he was even killed. But he did so much more than that. He showed us what life was intended to be like. He showed us what our lives could be if we were freed from the infection. Then Jesus gave us the antidote.

When we see Jesus' life, something resonates within us. It is readily apparent to almost everyone that the kind of life he lived is the kind of life we should live as well. You see, we are aware at different times and to different degrees that something is wrong with us. Just as the same cancer can metastasize at different rates in different bodies, the side effects of the sin infection can fluctuate in different people based on any number of factors. Some people, even though infected equally, see the side effects more clearly and strive to live lives free from them.

We know these people when we see them. Though not believers in the need for an antidote—or the infection itself—they are kinder, they are more willing to sacrifice for others, and they are more generous, more hopeful. Sometimes these differences come very naturally. Many times it takes discipline on their parts. They work hard to live well. They should be commended for this—often our lives are better for their presence in our lives or society in general. Sometimes they will take us under their wing and help us learn to live as they do. They may write books, allow us to join them for a weekend of training, or walk with us through years of our lives and share what they have learned with us.

Again, they almost always make our lives better, our world kinder. And we should be grateful to them.

But the lessons they have learned and the techniques they apply do nothing about the infection that continues to rage in our souls. Looking less infected and even very selflessly helping others to appear the same is not the same as not being infected. Intent isn't always enough.

How to Stop the Infection

Joseph Lister got that.

Joseph Lister was a Scottish surgeon in the mid-1800s. He was intrigued by Pasteur's discovery that germs multiply only after they are introduced to an atmosphere where they can grow. Up to this point, the theory of *spontaneous regeneration* was held to be true—germs would spontaneously form and there was essentially nothing that could be done about it. To Lister, a surgeon who, like his contemporaries, experienced a very high mortality rate in postsurgical patients, this was a fascinating discovery.[2]

Up to this point, surgeons would routinely operate on one patient and then another with almost no cleaning of their hands and instruments in between. They would perform autopsies and then operate on live patients with little cleaning as well. More recently they had started wiping their instruments on a towel or their aprons, but that towel or those aprons were the same ones they used all day. If Pasteur was right, Lister realized, all they were doing to try to prevent the spread of germs was useless. If Pasteur was right, then they weren't really doing anything to stop the spread of disease.[3]

Yes, they were trying. But up to this point they suspected it was the air itself that was the culprit, that air allowed for tissue breakdown and infection. And since you couldn't completely remove all the air from around a wound, things were pretty hopeless. Lister came to the conclusion that they were simply looking in the wrong place.

Lister realized something that is completely true of us in dealing with our soul infection. He realized that if the thing being relied on to clean oneself up is already infected, then the attempt to become clean is hopeless.

It is critical we understand this. Paul of Tarsus said in his letter to the church that had been started in Rome,

> Basically, all of us, whether insiders or outsiders, start out in identical conditions, which is to say that we all start out as sinners. Scripture leaves no doubt about it: There's nobody living right, not even one, nobody who knows the score, nobody alert for God. They've all taken the wrong turn; they've all wandered down blind alleys. No one's living right; I can't find a single one. (Romans 3:9–12 MSG)

God is making this very clear: we all are infected. Every one of us, even those who live as if they aren't. And even the best ideas for clearing up the infection, the best ideas for an antidote, are themselves infected because they come from infected minds. Just like those aprons skilled and caring surgeons wore: the physicians truly thought they were creating a safe, sterile atmosphere, but that didn't change the fact that they weren't. Simply put, we are incapable of clearing up this infection.

Our intentions might be wonderful, but either we deal with the infection or we don't. Nothing we make is clean and nothing we make has any capability of pushing the infection out of our souls, where it is reproducing constantly. There is no getting rid of it.

But this isn't the end of it. Jesus did the thing we couldn't. We can historically demonstrate that the Romans crucified Jesus of Nazareth and three days later he came back to life. In his doing that, he became our antidote. In those last moments of Jesus' life while he was on the cross, God the Father allowed the entirety of the infection and its side effects to be leveled at him. God threw it all on Jesus and Jesus died holding on to it. Either it was going to crush him under its weight or he would crush it. There would be no tie.

Jesus did the thing we couldn't.

We Need the Antidote

When our kids were younger, they loved watching the animated *Tarzan* movie. I cannot even hazard a guess at how many times we watched it. One part that almost always caused a hush in the room was when the evil leopard and Tarzan fell into a pit together. Remember that scene? The way they were going after each other, only one of them was going to come out of that pit. Seconds seemed like hours to my kids as they watched. First, to their horror, the shoulders and back of the leopard came up, then they screamed in victory when they saw that Tarzan was really the victor, tossing the dead body of the leopard to the ground. Its ability to harass and harm Tarzan's family was ended definitively.

The Resurrection was a bit like that. When Jesus died (which the Bible describes as going down into the pit), only he or sin was coming out the winner.

Three days later, when he rose from the dead, the victor was revealed. Jesus had conquered the infection. And in a crazy exchange, God allowed the blood he shed in that process to become the thing we were incapable of making for ourselves. His blood became our antidote. Because he was God and infection-free, he could truly give us something that was pure; because he was human, he was able to make it useful to us.

Jesus' blood became our antidote.

The best ideas for how to live without this antidote are, at best, like trying to treat the pain of brain cancer with an ice pack and some ibuprofen. Such actions are minimally helpful for the moment, but they do nothing to solve the problem that is causing the side effects. *This* antidote comes when we realize we need it. We take this antidote at a soul level by affirming that we need it and that Jesus' death and resurrection are the only sources of it. Then we tell God that we will seek to orient our lives around the example of Jesus and the reign of God.

When we acknowledge our need and desire for the antidote God provided, the Bible says our souls are immediately and permanently freed from the infection. God has shown us a way to be made right with him without keeping the requirements of the law (God has allowed us to get the antidote without our having to lead perfect lives to get it). *We are made right with God by placing our faith in Jesus Christ. And this is true for everyone who believes.*

If we ask Jesus to give us the antidote and acknowledge we

are incapable of making it on our own, then it doesn't matter how infected we are or what we have done because of the infection. God loves us enough to provide it for us. This allows God to honor our independence and let us make the choice to reconnect with him while, at the same time, making that reconnection something within everyone's reach.

From this point on we are no longer unavoidably tied to the side effects of the infection, but we still struggle with their legacy. Like the phantom pains some amputees deal with, we must deal with old habits that are hard to let go. We essentially begin relearning what life can be like without the infection in us. We learn how to look at people with uninfected eyes, not as sources of pain or pleasure for us, but as fellow creations of God; as people God longs to be with as much as he wants to be with us.

A Huge Risk

God's solution really is the only one that can work. We can choose to remain at odds with God. We can choose to create another version of God for ourselves or follow another version that makes more sense. God gives us that choice. As he did in the Garden, God gives us the option to do the wrong thing. But should we come to the realization that our ways are useless for truly curing the infection and reconciling us to God (as the Scriptures make clear, everyone is confronted with this reality in some manner), he makes the antidote very accessible.

**God's solution really is the only one that
can work.**

By far, this is the riskiest thing God could have done. And that gamble has already cost him dearly and will continue to do so. Remember back in the Garden? The tree that God asked Adam and Eve to stay away from? That tree symbolized our freedom and his risk. Offering the tree was risky for God because we could then choose the option of life in rebellion against him. We could use the freedom he had granted us to leave him and never come back.

God still risks today. And he handles the situation very similarly. When he was instructing Adam and Eve about the tree, he was clear about everything that was at stake should they go for it. In the same way, he is clear with us. As I've said, if he forced us to believe and accept the antidote, then our presence with him wouldn't be chosen, and we would be imprisoned with him. So, he predicates our antidote on faith, on believing what we cannot fully see. If we are willing to allow him, he leads us right up to it, but it is always in the end our choice. Do we take the antidote, and by doing so, acknowledge his reality and his right to guide our lives? Do we give up our belief that we can conjure up something that will rid us of this infection?

The benefits for taking the antidote are not limited to our lives here on earth—and neither are the risks of refusing. The closeness we will enjoy with God when he eradicates the infection from the entire planet simply cannot coexist with our infected souls. To be with God after our deaths, we must have asked to receive the antidote. Upon our deaths, out of necessity, God honors whatever decision we made about him. If we have asked for the antidote in our lives, we walk into the reality of that decision after death and go to be with God in heaven. If we spend our lives indicating to God that we prefer to be separated from him, he very sadly acknowledges that, and upon our deaths, that decision is also locked in and we are separated from him for eternity.

What a terrible risk for the God who loves us more than we could ever love even those closest to us. Each one of us is named and cared for, either reluctantly from afar or joyously from within.

Each one of us is named and cared for, either reluctantly from afar or joyously from within.

Back to the Field

My wife and I run that risk with our children: Try to force them to love us, and that love will never be real. Give them the room to roam a bit and love us on their own, and they may never choose to do so. But our job as parents requires that we stare down that fear and not give in. We have to do what is right even at the risk of great personal cost. We have to be willing to do what is required for the good of our kids and trust they will not leave us for having done it.

That is why Noah had to go out into the outfield that day. Even though both of us would have preferred not to.

But as Noah walked to that outfield, I went with him so that, if nothing else, he could know that his dad wasn't ashamed of being associated with him. I just stood near him, just past the foul line. Sometimes he would look up at me in gratitude, sometimes in anger that he had to take the field at all, and at other times during those innings, I think he forgot I was there entirely.

But in those moments, I got something much more precious than the reassurance I was giving. I was shown how a love greater than I will ever understand could restrain itself because something much larger was going on. In the midst of the difficulty, God in his love isn't staying far away, isn't distracting himself to make this stage of his plan easier on himself. He is right here with each of us, sometimes very near, but never far away, and always watching us with a true father's love.

Through my oldest son's baseball difficulties, I learned a bit about what it is like to have the ability to remove the suffering of someone you deeply love, but because of a larger issue that your loved one doesn't understand, needing to deny yourself the use of that ability. God understands that fear because he lives in the reality of that risk too. I learned I am not the only one with a lot on the table.

Questions for Reflection and Discussion

1. Have you ever had to limit your use of available power in a situation for the purpose of a greater good? What was that situation?

2. Do you see why God might need to limit his authority and power for our good? As you reflect on that, what do you think about?

3. How does Jesus' fictitious story of the father and his two sons that is included in Luke chapter 15 describe God the Father's approach to us?

4. Do you understand that the father was risking his entire relationship in not pursuing his son and making him come home? Does that frustrate you? If so, what do you think would have been the result had the father forced his son to come home before he was ready?

5. If we understand that the father in the parable is representing God the Father, what are the implications for a father who truly loves his children when those children aren't sure they want anything to do with him?

6. Do you see the infection that either you still have or (if you have asked Jesus to be your antidote) you once had? Do you see the remaining side effects that you carry? What are your most present ones?

7. Do you see the impossibility on your part to provide your own antidote?

7

God's Approach to Our Protection

You know people are passionate when they spit a little when they are talking. You know they are passionately *angry* when you, and they, see the spittle fly out of their mouths, land on your cheek—and they just keep going. In my case, the person paused a second, saw me wipe my cheek off, and then continued railing on God and on me for disagreeing with him.

Now, I didn't start this. I was in a coffee shop, and the mad spitter was in a conversation about God with someone else. The person he was in the conversation with saw me and pulled me in. I have often learned that the phrase "Hey, I think that dude works for a church" doesn't bode well for how the person feels about the church, and by default, me. And as angry as this guy was, I could understand where he was coming from.

I think that an awful lot of the time people become very frustrated with one another because they disagree about how involved in some difficult situation someone should be. But the type of ferocity that was causing my unexpected salivary shower in that coffee shop can be caused by other things as well. One that matters here is when someone is behaving in an unexpected way. I have seen some pretty big fights and relational fissures form as a result of things being done unexpectedly when a lot is on the line. That has been happening in the church for as long as there has been one. Let's take a look at a couple of issues that made people mad spitters.

Meat: It Mattered—a Lot

The early Christians' view of meat, their use of it, where they got it, and what they did with it mattered; in their culture, it mattered a lot.

Not the way it matters for us. Cholesterol wasn't an issue; they rarely ate enough to have problems with heart disease. It had nothing to do with the amount of marbling of the fat, what types of grain the animals were fed, or how the meat was prepared. Meat was an issue on a whole different level for them.

And God really began to up the pressure on this issue one day when Peter had a vision. It all went down in Acts 10. Realize this was several years after Jesus had been resurrected, and the church was just getting going. Peter was praying on a rooftop and God gave him a vision, in which Peter saw the sky "open up, and something like a large sheet was let down by its four corners. In the sheet were all sorts of animals, reptiles, and birds. Then a voice said to him, 'Get up, Peter; kill and eat them'" (Acts 10:11–13 NLT).

This would have been as strange for Peter and his fellow Jews as it would be for us today. Imagine a platter with several reptiles on it and you're told you can eat them. Sound good? Personally, short of Cajun 'gator poppers, my experience with eating reptiles is somewhat shallow, and trying a bunch of things I had never considered food would be tough. Peter probably had a hard time imagining eating the pigs that were on the sheet he saw. But there was a lot more to it than just what looked good.

Imagine a platter with several reptiles on it and you're told you can eat them. Sound good?

In the last chapter we saw that over the history of God's special relationship with the Jews, God had certain rules in place. Many of these existed to continually demonstrate to the Jews that God had a role in every single part of their lives. Part of this law included certain dietary restrictions.

These restrictions weren't general guides. Many were very specific and they were important. You kept them. You didn't violate them without penalty. If you lived back then, you would have known what food was acceptable and what was not. You would have thought about food in terms of "clean" and "unclean." Clean foods you could dig into—unclean foods you were commanded to leave alone.

What if in a prayer time you felt God saying he wanted you to begin enjoying different foods than you had previously experienced? You might think, *Hey—finally a reason to give papaya a shot!* But that is not what Peter would have been thinking. To get a bit more into Peter's head, imagine if God commanded you to nosh down on a Goliath-size tarantula. Those things can grow to over eleven inches, can have fangs an inch long, and can catch mice and even small birds! Imagine God telling you that you were free to serve them up.

Now imagine he told you to start eating!

What you're feeling now is probably close to what Peter felt: confused and more than a bit grossed out. If God gave you the same message, you would understand why God had to give the vision three times to get Peter on board. And very quickly we see what God was really up to: shifting to an *all foods are clean* system was just the preparation for an even more critical *all people are clean* way of life. I bet when Peter started talking up the new rules to die-hard Jews, some spittle was hitting his cheek, eh?

A Way of Life

To the very earliest believers in Jesus, following him didn't mean leaving the law behind. It was woven into the fabric of the Jews' lives. Jesus was the Messiah, the Jews were the chosen people of God, and the guidelines were still in place.

But as in all systems, there were some gray areas. Beyond what meat you ate, in the early church, where you got the meat you did eat was an issue. In that day, animal sacrifice was used as a part of idol worship. Then those temples would sell their meat at the markets. It would be cheaper than other meat you could buy, so it was a bargain. But it brought with it some problems.

When Paul, the church planter and leader, wrote one of his letters to the church in the city of Corinth, he dealt with the topic:

> What about eating meat that has been offered to idols? Well, we all know that an idol is not really a god and that there is only one God. There may be so-called gods both in heaven and on earth, and some people actually worship many gods and many lords. But we know that there is only one God, the Father, who created everything, and we live for him. And there is only one Lord, Jesus Christ, through whom God made everything and through whom we have been given life. However, not all believers know this. Some are accustomed to thinking of idols as being real, so when they eat food that has been offered to idols, they think of it as the worship of real gods, and their weak consciences are violated. It's true that we can't win God's approval by what we eat. We don't lose anything if we don't eat it, and we don't gain anything if we do. (1 Corinthians 8:4–8 NLT)

Paul dealt with this issue a number of times in the early years of the church. As completely unimportant as it would appear to be to us, both the "It's okay to eat that meat" and "It's definitely not okay to eat that meat" groups believed themselves to be right.

Here is a key reason they couldn't agree and resolve the issue: they were missing the point. They were making a physical matter out of what was a spiritual matter.

They were making a physical matter out of what was a spiritual matter.

For the non-Jews (Gentiles) who followed Jesus, eating meat offered to idols was no big deal. Gentiles had never had these restrictions and felt little need to take up what many of them saw as unnecessary Jewish restrictiveness. To them, all foods were perfectly fine to consume.

Another Rite Hard to Give Up

This conflict continued beyond the issue of food. And as you could probably guess, more spittle was spread in those issues as well. God seemed to be intent on expanding the Jewish Christians' view of what he was doing. Surprisingly enough, one of the tougher pieces of their heritage to give up was the tradition of circumcision. In the book of Acts, which records many of the exploits of the early church, we see Paul and Barnabas (another early church planter and leader) run headlong into this issue:

While Paul and Barnabas were at Antioch of Syria, some men from Judea arrived and began to teach the believers: "Unless you are circumcised as required by the law of Moses, you cannot be saved." Paul and Barnabas disagreed with them, arguing vehemently. Finally, the church decided to send Paul and Barnabas to Jerusalem, accompanied by some local believers, to talk to the apostles and elders about this question. The church sent the delegates to Jerusalem, and they stopped along the way in Phoenicia and Samaria to visit the believers. They told them—much to everyone's joy—that the Gentiles, too, were being converted. When they arrived in Jerusalem, Paul and Barnabas were welcomed by the whole church, including the apostles and elders. They reported everything God had done through them. But then some of the believers who belonged to the sect of the Pharisees stood up and insisted, "The Gentile converts must be circumcised and required to follow the law of Moses." (Acts 15:1–5 NLT)

Say what?

Conflict arose around the tradition of an infant male having his foreskin removed by a mohel. A good mohel (and you really didn't want a bad one) could remove the foreskin in two or three flicks of his flint knife. The extended family would attend this rite; in fact, in orthodox families this was a very meaningful ceremony. You wouldn't even conduct the ceremony without at least ten adult men attending. Following the circumcision, the boy would be given his Hebrew name.

This act was a profound part of who the Jews were culturally and as such was very hard to let go of. But you can certainly understand the drive of an adult Gentile, an uncircumcised man, to see if this was *really* a necessary step to take!

To be fair, circumcision and the Jews went way back. All the way to Abraham, in fact. In Genesis 17, as God explained the special relationship he would have with the Jews, he instituted this very personal and permanent marking. And from there the people mostly maintained the covenant. It isn't tough to see why the Jews felt it was such an important part of their heritage. It was a very personal reflection of their being a part of the people of Yahweh. Circumcision, dietary restrictions, obeying the celebration of certain feasts throughout the year, sacrifices: these spoke to who you were—whose you were. And you didn't just let centuries-old traditions and laws go.

Conflicts Old and New

But in the days of the early church, Paul was suggesting just that. He was making the case that followers of Jesus didn't need to practice those traditions. I remember how heated it got about ten years ago when we decided to change the name of our student ministry. People got *hot*. I cannot begin to imagine how intense some of these religious discussions were. Acts 15:2 says that the discussions were characterized by "sharp dispute and debate" (NIV). Maybe some more spittle?

But in the end, circumcision was over. It wasn't necessary anymore. Things had changed.

Today, we don't agree with one another very much about God. Even within the Protestant world we have significant disagreements. Are we making becoming a follower of Jesus too easy—or are we setting the bar too high? Are we just accepting at face value the way of connecting with Christ that our parents taught us? What parts of the Bible do you like most, the Gospels or the Epistles? Is it okay for Wal-Mart to sell Jesus action figures or for us to wear shirts that tell everyone "Jesus Is My Homeboy"? In the WWJD ("What Would Jesus Do?") and the FROG ("Fully Rely on God") silicon-band wars, who is right? Alcohol: right or wrong? Should a Christian tithe on his lottery winnings or is it best to not let people know that you have been gambling? How seriously should the prayer of Jabez be taken?

Those conflicts reveal what we believe to be Jesus' intentions with us.

We have our own set of issues that go with our faith in God, and we can argue seriously over them. If we are to look at the various issues that can cause disagreement and compare them to those our Jewish brothers and sisters faced a couple of thousand years ago, the conflicts seem to have little in common. But there is much more than we might initially suspect. And those conflicts reveal what we believe to be Jesus' intentions with us. They also deal with his methods. It can be as frustrating now as it was for the Jewish followers of Jesus then.

Lessons Learned from Superheroes

Bear with me as we take on the subject of God's intentions by examining an unexpected source: superheroes. They need no more introduction; we all know what they are.

Superheroes are a funny thing to us. When we are first introduced to them we want them to be truly super—to have out-of-this-world powers that originate, well, outside of this world. We want the heroes' parents to have strange names, and if the heroes can wear a cape or the ubiquitous silver unitard, all the better. Something in us wants to be protected by a powerful hero. We want to know that even if it looks as if there is no hope, we will hear a whooshing sound and be pulled to safety.

We want to know that even if it looks as if there is no hope, we will hear a whooshing sound and be pulled to safety.

Still, pretty soon we grow bored with superheroes' abilities, and their creators have to start showing us how human they really are. Superman struggles with the loss of Lois Lane and eventually gives up his power for a time to be with her. Spider-Man decides he wants a normal life with Mary Jane. The Fantastic Four? The same. They all struggle with the celebrity that their power brings, either loving it too much or hating it. Even the Incredibles struggle with the realities of their superpowers. And all of the superheroes go through that seemingly necessary phase when they tune out our cries for help in favor of less-powerful lives.

Probably no superhero demonstrates this better than Will Smith's depiction of Hancock, someone with incredible power that seems to come at incredible cost. He is a hero we can be more comfortable with: he's as flawed, or even more so, than we are.

But we want our superheroes to eventually snap out of any state of mind that might cause them to have less than full access to their powers, right? They realize in their fictitious worlds what we are already certain of in ours: that if you can help, you should. If you have extraordinary power, then you use it to help those who don't. In the real world, we even have Good Samaritan laws in some states that require us to step in and help if we can. Watching preventable pain unfold without taking action is not considered a mark of restraint, or wisdom, or concern for the larger good. We don't classify it as "seeing the bigger picture." We see it as selfish and wrong.

Many people look at God that way. He is up "there" in heaven, with a courtside view of the devastation. Maybe he's just sitting on his hands while it all happens, or worse, he's causing it himself. God starts to look pretty cruel. And once again, the questions return: does he not stop the damage because he isn't strong enough or because he doesn't care enough?

Does he not stop the damage because he isn't strong enough or because he doesn't care enough?

Or is it that he isn't real enough? And we even argue over which of those reasons is really true.

Back to What God Should Be Up To

Out of all this disagreement, there is one thing almost everyone agrees on, whether or not they even believe in God: if he (or she or it) is real, he needs to protect us.

In many ways, in our culture today, God's protection is like the meat issue of the early church. Strong opinions and harsh words come from both sides. How much protecting would God be doing if he was real and/or doing a good job at being God?

In almost any survey where respondents are asked about what is most important for God to be doing, consistently number one or two is some variant of "God should protect us." In their book *Soul Searching: The Religious and Spiritual Lives of American Teenagers*, Christian Smith and Melinda Lundquist Denton note this very thing. The teenagers surveyed agreed that a central function and desire of God was that they be protected and happy.[1] That isn't new. It has almost always been that way with the supernatural. Entire mythologies have been developed for the purposes of those following them to feel safe and protected in a world that offers neither safety nor protection.

In most countries in the developed world that are not in the midst of war, protection isn't something people are grateful for overall. In the United States, our level of gratitude has become low. We have been relatively safe for so long that our protection has become an expectation.

Once again, this creates a problem with God and us. It's not just that we feel we need to be protected; to deliberately refrain from protecting someone you have the ability to protect is offensive to us. And God seems to be really dropping the ball on this one. The question is, which is right? Is he really dropping it? Or does it just seem as though he is?

I think God's answer to this issue might surprise us a bit. He talked about what a life of faith can look like in Hebrews 11. A holy life can look as you would expect it to—full of wonderful things that only God can do. And it can also look as you wouldn't expect it to—with fair and faith-filled requests going long unanswered and various harms being suffered. In the letter to the church in Rome, Paul asks, "Does it mean he no longer loves us if we have trouble or calamity, or are persecuted, or hungry, or destitute, or in danger, or threatened with death?" (Romans 8:35 NLT). God would agree that he is not protecting us as much as we—and interestingly, he—would like. But he might disagree that our physical protection is job one.

A holy life can look as you wouldn't expect it to—with fair and faith-filled requests going long unanswered.

God's Track Record of Protecting People

God—who raised not only Lazarus from death, but also a boy who got so bored with what Paul was saying that he fell out of a high window and died—didn't always do the same with the closest disciples of Jesus.

- James the Great, the elder brother of John the Apostle, was beheaded in AD 44.
- Philip, who served in Upper Asia, was scourged in Phrygia, thrown into prison, and later crucified (AD 54).
- Matthew the tax collector served the Lord in Parthia and Ethiopia where he was slain with a halberd (a shafted weapon with an ax-like cutting blade and a speared end) in the city of Nadabah (AD 60).
- James the Less, the brother of the Lord, served the church in Jerusalem and wrote the book of James. He suffered martyrdom at the age of ninety-four by being beaten and stoned by the Jews.
- Matthias, the man who was chosen to replace Judas as an apostle, was stoned at Jerusalem and then beheaded.
- Andrew, the brother of Peter, preached the gospel to many Asiatic nations and was crucified on a cross at Edessa. The ends of his cross were fixed transversely in the ground, thus the derivation of the term "Saint Andrew's cross."
- Mark was converted to Christianity by Peter and served as his amanuensis (he wrote for Peter). He was dragged to pieces by the people of Alexandria.

- Peter the Apostle was sought by Nero to be put to death. Jerome wrote that Peter was crucified with his head down and his feet up because he thought himself unworthy to be crucified in the same form and manner as the Lord.
- Paul was persecuted several times. He was scourged, stoned, and, finally, Nero had him beheaded with a sword.
- Jude, the brother of James, commonly called Thaddeus, was crucified at Edessa in AD 72.
- Bartholomew preached in several countries and translated the Gospel of Matthew into the language of India. He was cruelly beaten and then crucified by impatient idolaters.
- Thomas (the doubting one) preached the gospel in Parthia and India. He excited the rage of the pagan priests and was martyred by being thrust through with a spear.
- Luke, the author of Luke and Acts, traveled with Paul through various countries and was supposed to have been hanged on an olive tree by the idolatrous priests of Greece.
- Simon the Zealot preached the gospel in Mauritania, Africa, and even Britain, where he was crucified in AD 74.
- John, "the apostle whom Jesus loved," was sent from Ephesus to Rome where he was put into a cauldron of boiling oil. He escaped without injury by a miracle but was then banished to the Isle of Patmos and there he wrote the book of Revelation. Nerva, Domitian's successor, said he was the only apostle who escaped a violent death.[2]

Wow. God doesn't seem to have a very good track record of protecting people.

What God Doesn't Promise

If we look carefully, we can see a thread that seems to weave throughout God's approach to us. It isn't that he promises to protect us from the terror of this world; however, it finds its way to our door. In many cases he does protect us, and likely only a few times are we even aware of what he has done. Amy Grant once recorded a song that talks about a "reckless car [that] ran out of gas" before it hurt anyone. That kind of stuff.

But if we are honest, most of us think he doesn't intervene enough. For every story of a child saved there seem to be ten about a child lost. For every healing, how many funerals? For every near-miss, how many collisions? I have many friends who have served in Iraq and Afghanistan, and almost every one has come back with banged-up faith. War isn't like the original *Star Trek* episodes where if Kirk, Spock, or McCoy beamed into a dangerous situation with a random, unnamed crew member, well, you could guess who was going to get the worst of it. Nope, real war is seemingly much more random. No way to tell until it happens. Maybe you would be the one hurt or killed, maybe not.

**If we are honest, most of us think he doesn't
intervene enough.**

In the same way, there was no way to predict before April 16 upon which occupants of which building Cho would unleash his anger. It could have been any of them.

Once again, we are left up against the hard and cold wall of the question of what can be expected from God. If so many of us agree that he should be our protector, why doesn't he listen to the people and protect?

But remember, he seems to think he does. How could that be?

Through *Rather Than* From

God would say he is protecting us *through*, rather than *from*, the difficulties of our world. This isn't because he doesn't care about us, or because he is lazy and just won't get moving, or because his office is vacant. It's because the plan he has in place requires it. We talked about this earlier. To protect us as fully as we would prefer would require that he step in and assume control of whoever was about to hurt someone. What if the charge we have leveled at him all this time has been coming from the wrong direction?

God would say he is protecting us *through*, rather than *from*, the difficulties of our world.

What if the very clear pain he allows doesn't occur due to his absence or weakness, but rather out of necessity? Look at what God the Son, Jesus, says in the most famous of his marching orders given just before he ascended to heaven in front of hundreds of his followers about forty days after his resurrection.

We call it the Great Commission, the challenge of challenges, the task at hand. And right at the tail end of it we see his approach:

> The eleven disciples were on their way to Galilee, headed for the mountain Jesus had set for their reunion. The moment they saw him they worshiped him. Some, though, held back, not sure about worship, about risking themselves totally. Jesus, undeterred, went right ahead and gave his charge: "God authorized and commanded me to commission you: Go out and train everyone you meet, far and near, in this way of life, marking them by baptism in the threefold name: Father, Son, and Holy Spirit. Then instruct them in the practice of all I have commanded you. I'll be with you as you do this, day after day after day, right up to the end of the age." (Matthew 28:16–20 MSG)

Here, right at the end of Jesus' time on earth, he tells his followers how to continue what he instituted. He said to go everywhere and help everyone we meet to understand the truth of his reality. But it is the very end of this commission that we should look more closely at: here Jesus tells his followers that while they are doing this, *he will be with them, day after day after day, right up until the very end.* God is not absent or weak or uncaring. He is protecting us in a different way. He doesn't always protect us *from*, but we can be certain he does always guide us *through*.

He makes no promise that everything will go well, but he absolutely declares that once we invite him into our lives, he will walk with us through everything that could ever come up.

Picture the scene just before the Jewish leaders took Jesus to his execution. It was the same issue we face, just on a larger level: where was God's protection? God the Son, Jesus, was scared, if not terrified. He knew how awful it would be to have the entirety of the world's rebellion for all time leveled at him, how repugnant that would be. And I bet he also knew how badly it would hurt.

Remember my dislocated shoulder? After my injury, I had some physical therapy done on it, but it needed surgery to really heal. So, every now and then, it would get pulled out of the socket. And sometimes it hurt so much it brought tears to my eyes. I had become very aware of what could make it go out of the socket and really tried to avoid those movements. That stabbing pain felt as if something was grinding against something it shouldn't be grinding against in there. I hated that feeling. Knowing how much it would hurt was a big influence on what I would do. I very much didn't want to feel that pain.

And that would have been nothing like what Jesus felt. I bet he knew how it would feel, or at least had a good idea, and that was part of why he was so scared. Crucifixions were common in Jesus' day, as were the scourgings that were typically administered before the actual crucifixion. God didn't protect him from the Crucifixion, or the mocking and beatings that preceded it. As he was in his life and ministry, Jesus continued to be our example. In this case, there was no avoiding it, God walked

Jesus through it. Sometimes he cannot save us *from* pain; he has promised to be our companion *through* it.

God didn't protect him from the Crucifixion, or the mocking and beatings that preceded it.

Want another example? Look at the story of the church at Philippi.

Paul wrote a letter to the church at Philippi while he was serving under Roman house arrest. This letter is strongly focused on peace and joy, on how God will be with us in all things and we need to realize that when we become followers of Jesus, we become citizens of heaven. We still have very active and important lives here on earth, but the hope for our lives shifts to heaven. If things don't ever get better here on earth, they will get better for us in heaven. *That* becomes the hope God intends to be part of our fuel for following him here.

As for life on earth, Paul wrote, "Don't worry about anything; instead, pray about everything. Tell God what you need, and thank him for all he has done. Then you will experience God's peace, which exceeds anything we can understand. His peace will guard your hearts and minds as you live in Christ Jesus" (Philippians 4:6–7 NLT).

God isn't hiding anything. He put the truth right in front of our faces. He tells us through the words he gave to Paul that our focus should be on talking to God about everything in our lives...rather than on a false expectation of his continual protection from all harm. When we consistently communicate with him, we gain access to a peace that doesn't make sense given our circumstances—it exceeds anything we can understand.

And the Philippian church was going to desperately need that to be true.

In just a couple of years they were going to go through the ringer.

Philippi in the Crosshairs

The main means of dating this letter to the church in Philippi is in Paul's mention of his imprisonment and the question of whether or not he will survive. Unfortunately for us, and even more so for Paul, he was imprisoned more than once! The traditional view is that Paul penned this letter around AD 59–63. Anytime in that range put the Philippian followers of Jesus literally in front of the mouth of a cannon—they just didn't realize it yet.

But God did.

In AD 64 a fire broke out in the merchant section of the city of Rome. It was fanned by the strong summer winds and the dry wood of that section of the city. By the time the fire was put out six days later, 70 percent of the city was a burned ruin. The Great Fire of Rome had earned its title.[3]

And someone had to be blamed.

Nero, the emperor of that day, has been widely believed to have started the fire to burn out the ugly sections of Rome he wanted to rebuild. Unfortunately, not even the rocking-cool CSI team members of Las Vegas (I think we all would agree the ones in Miami are lamer) could go back and determine beyond the shadow of a doubt who did it. But we can be absolutely certain who was blamed for it. Nero blamed it on the Christians. This kicked off one of the most difficult periods of persecution for those who truly had done nothing other than decide to follow the Messiah.

The church at Philippi would be especially impacted by this for a couple of reasons. First, there was a small number of Christians in the city (there were not even the ten families that were necessary, according to the Torah, to start a synagogue); and second, the citizens of Philippi gave high allegiance to Rome. This was mostly due to the Roman military's retirement plan for higher-ranking soldiers and officers. Instead of getting a lifetime pension or some sweet 401(k) action, many retirees received land. Philippi was a key place where the land was given. This gave the retirees a means to support themselves after their periods of service were finished. The Roman government would typically do this in areas that would otherwise be hard to defend against attack. So you had seasoned and grateful soldiers in areas where seasoned and grateful soldiers probably came in very handy.

Also, Philippi could trace its heritage back to King Phillip, the father of Alexander the Great. Today, most of us would have a hard time supplying information concerning the origin of our city's or town's name. (Our friends in Washington, D.C., are excluded from this group.) The heritage of our cities doesn't tend to be a big deal for us, but it was for the Philippians. They heavily aligned themselves with Rome, and they were very proud of the heritage of their city, so when the fire hit they were upset. Their favorite city was in ruins. But they were more than upset, or sad—they were offended. It was as if they themselves had been attacked. They likely felt the same way many of us did when we watched in horror as the Twin Towers fell in New York City: saddened, and ready to get back at whoever did it. So when Nero blamed the Christians, the people of Philippi made those believers who lived around them pay.

And the Christians did pay, all over the empire. Nero was known equally for his beautiful architecture and his horrific creativity in killing people. A number of historians describe him, in just one example, as ordering Christians to be hung on poles, after which he had them wrapped in rope soaked in pitch and wax. Then he gave the order to light them on fire. The pitch kept the rope and the victims burning while the wax ensured they didn't burn too fast. Stories of Nero riding his chariot around his gardens at night with the only light coming from that grotesque scene were common.[4]

Guess what else?

God saw it all coming. But look at the letter God the Holy Spirit led Paul to write. What did he say? "Run"? Where could they run? At this point in history, Rome was functionally everywhere. How do you escape when the enemy is truly all around you?

God could have supernaturally whisked the Philippians away to somewhere else safe, but if he did that, would he have to do that every time? If he eradicated the evil in the world at that point, we would have never had a chance at life. The operation required would be so invasive that it would kill us. The rebellion, the sin, that leads to such massive atrocity is not separate from us; it is bound up in us, in our souls. Once again, the thing that often limits God's ability to intervene is his desire for us to have a chance at living. His awareness that the time isn't yet right to call an end to the terror that we now, and the Philippian Christians then, walk in daily.

The thing that often limits God's ability to intervene is his desire for us to have a chance at living.

It doesn't seem as if Paul knew what was coming, but God did. And God wasn't rendered powerless by the force of the Roman Empire, wasn't cowed by what would have been terrifying to any person living then. He didn't stop the onslaught, but watch what he did.

He got them ready.

Paul wrote the Philippians about considering the example of Jesus, who himself endured unjust abuse. He encouraged them to give all their concerns to him, to pray about everything. Paul told them that they had not only the privilege of trusting in Christ, but also the privilege of suffering for him. He told them to not look at what was behind them, but to strain heavenward for what was to come. In short, he prepared them for suffering.

God still operates that way: protecting us not always from, but constantly through, trouble.

In Modern-Day Suffering

In the aftermath of the Virginia Tech shootings, story after story came from reliable people who described clear leading from God to pray for people who were later killed or injured. One guy told me that out of the blue on April 14, he felt a need to pray that a woman who was walking by him would accept Christ's antidote. For this guy, praying in such a direct way for someone just walking by him, among the dozens of people he saw in a given day, was unusual. He burned that image of the woman onto his brain and kept praying for her. Two days after the shootings he was looking at the photos of those killed and realized one of them was the very person he had been guided to pray for just four days before.

People have shared stories of feeling a need to pray for Virginia Tech in the days and weeks preceding the shootings. Even our church went through a season of preparation. Only a couple of weeks before the shootings, I made the comment to some of our staff that things had been unusually stable. (Imagine a church of close to a thousand twenty- and thirty-somethings in the midst of starting a new congregation in the same city, as well as a new church three hours away, and you can understand why *stable* would stick out.) We also noticed that our small groups had been through a season of strengthening and were being led by God in strong ways. We saw those outward things but had no idea what we were being prepared for.

We had no idea that those groups, led almost exclusively by people in their twenties and early thirties, many also being fairly new followers of Jesus, would need to navigate their members through a tragedy that would indelibly mark everyone associated with our church for the rest of their lives.

Did God Say, "Enough!"?

Want to know something that still bugs me? God could have dropped Cho dead of a heart attack that morning. He could have stopped Cho before he ever made it to Norris Hall. He could have allowed him to be arrested.

I will be honest. I still get angry with God about that sometimes. Not as much as I did in the immediate aftermath, but I still go through it.

God could have dropped Cho dead of a heart attack that morning.

At the same time, police reports indicate that Cho took his own life with more bullets left to use. That confuses me. He clearly showed no concern for people's lives when he walked or shoved or shot his way into a classroom, and he shot almost everyone in the face. He wasn't yet being challenged by the police. Why stop?

I wonder if at that point God said, *"Enough!"* No one can be sure, of course, but it is strange that Cho stopped before he was forced to by running out of ammunition.

I wonder if Cho's not being caught earlier, his being allowed to commit such a horror, and his possibly being restrained from unleashing everything he could have is a good metaphor for God's approach against evil for now: Sometimes he is able to intervene. And sometimes he must watch too. And weep with us.

Questions for Reflection and Discussion

1. What causes spit-laden conversations in your life?

2. What are the "meat" issues in your life, in your church (if you have one), or in your family or neighborhood?

3. If you had been alive when Peter was announcing his vision of the animals on the sheet lowered from heaven, how do you think you would have responded? Do you tend to be willing to let God be unpredictable or do you prefer that his interactions with you fit into a stable pattern?

4. Do you equate God's demonstration of his love for you with his demonstration of protection of you? How does Romans 8:35–39 factor into this view?

Who shall separate us from the love of Christ? Shall trouble or hardship or persecution or famine or nakedness or danger or sword?...No, in all these things we are more than conquerors through him who loved us. For I am convinced that neither death nor life, neither angels nor demons, neither the present nor the future, nor any powers, neither height nor depth, nor anything else in all creation, will be able to separate us from the love of God that is in Christ Jesus our Lord. (NIV)

5. Have you ever seen God walk you or someone else *through* difficulty instead of protecting you *from* it? What did that do to your trust in him? Why?

8

Where Was God That Day?

- "He should have been in class. Thank God he wasn't!"
- "I would have been in Norris Hall, right in the middle of all of it."
- "Why did God protect me and not the others?"
- "Why didn't he protect my friend who was shot in the hip, or my friend who was killed?"
- "Where was God when all this happened?"

The questions that hover just below the surface of all these questions, which I heard often in the months after the shooting and have heard after other tragedies, again, are simple to articulate but much more complicated to answer. "Where was God on April 16 [or September 11, or the day of the fire, or the day you learned your friend had been killed or the day your parents separated]? *Where is God in all our pain? And why doesn't he do more about it?*

It's a feeling like a dull cramp, and many of those affected by the shootings cannot turn it off. Nor should they blindly try. When a ship runs aground and dumps millions of barrels of oil into one of our oceans, or when an airplane unexpectedly nose-dives to the ground, our first questions are: "Where was the captain? Why didn't he do something?" It's a natural response to a calamity.

We know that if any one of us were up there looking down from God's vantage point on Virginia Tech on April 16, we would have gotten in the game. We would have done something.

If God is really who he claims to be, then we should be able to pose this question to him: "Where were you, God?"

Past Performance as a Key Predictor

It is a well-known and timeworn adage: "Past performance is a key predictor of future performance." Employers want to know how things have gone in your past work experience to determine how well you will do for them. College grades matter to future employers and graduate programs. It's why we get references before we let someone work on our houses, our cars, or us. And in many cases, we cannot work for someone until he or she checks our references. It is why at our church we recommend people interested in starting romantic relationships to really watch the persons they're interested in with their friends. How a person conducts friendships is a good indicator of how he or she will conduct a romance. The past can be a key determiner of what the future will look like.

The past can be a key determiner of what the future will look like.

We get this, don't we? As we went through adolescence, most of us used that very thought as our rallying cry: "Trust me, Mom and Dad! Let me show you I can make good choices!" And if you were anything like I was, you certainly always did. (Ha!)

Any of us involved in the lives of kids have felt this too. Tracy and I have observed each of our children when they didn't realize we were watching. We've seen them confront challenges and have the chance to choose the right decision or the wrong one. If you have been there, you know how great it feels when your child chooses to do the right thing. You feel elated not just because they made the right choice, but because they made the right choice *on their own*. They didn't do it to appease you or to submit to you, but because they have personally internalized the ideals you taught them and are living according to those values.

I remember a day in particular when my fairly quiet nine-year-old daughter came home and told me how she had included a girl new to the class in her group of friends. She was just doing it to be nice and seemed surprised when Tracy and I went crazy praising her! She had decided to do the uncomfortable thing so that the new little girl would be more comfortable.

These are some of the very pinnacle moments of life, when someone who doesn't have to choose you and your ways does so out of the desire of his or her heart. Powerful stuff.

God feels that too. And if the Garden of Eden had included only lots of great things for us to choose, there would be none of those moments. We would be robbed of our choice and our humanity, and God would be robbed of the opportunity to meaningfully guide us, love us, relate to us, and watch us walk with him of our own volition.

With only good trees in the Garden, we wouldn't have been better off. Actually much worse. God knew that.

With only good trees in the Garden, we wouldn't have been better off.... God knew that.

A Broken Record

The rest of the Old Testament shows, time and again, how God's people rejected his leadership or guidance and chose to go their own way. Or they got tired of him, they just forgot about him, or, once again, they started to wonder if he was holding out.

If you carefully read through the accounts of God's relationship with people, you can see how patient he is. Consider, for example, how God *responds* once Adam and Eve have messed up. First, there are clear consequences of their rebellion that God has to enforce: both the man and the woman will experience harder lives as a result of this choice. And the process that will lead to their physical death has begun. But then, in this very tender moment, you don't see God crush them in anger or burn them up with his wrath or his frustration. Instead, you see him make clothes for them to wear to hide their nakedness now that they are ashamed to be seen by God and each other that way.

We see this same tenderness even in those parts of the Bible that are really tough to read, the parts where God allows or even causes famine or military overthrow. No getting around it: he really does those things. But if you pay attention, you see that God doesn't blindly lash out in anger. He always gives guidelines that, as the Creator of everything, he is entitled to issue. He warns his people again and again and allows the really awful stuff only when nothing else has worked.

He always gives guidelines that, as the Creator of everything, he is entitled to issue.

I really don't like those parts of the Scriptures, but they are there. And as I have looked more closely, what I see is patience. Even in those moments when the consequences are significant, never does God remove from us the free will that we so clearly show we cannot really handle very well. There must be something pretty important for us to see there.

Jesus' Record

Skip forward several thousand years, and you come to the greatest indication of God's love for us. We need to take a look at God the Son, Jesus. Now, stay with me here. This part really matters.

To get this, you have to remember something we talked about earlier. God the Father, God the Son (Jesus), and God the Holy Spirit are all God: all equally God and distinct at the same time. This concept is called the doctrine of the Trinity. Each member of the Trinity has different functions, but they all have equal importance. None of them would be considered "less God" or the "JV God." Simply put: God essentially has community with himself. Hard to grasp? It is. But God is so much more advanced than we are, it is real.

When God the Son, Jesus, came to earth and was born, God came to earth—literally. But not the entirety of God. God the Father and God the Holy Spirit remained in heaven.

God the Son was born and lived a life that was perfect. He lived as God would. Jesus interacted with people, loved them, challenged them, laughed with them, and healed them. Simply put, he *enjoyed* them. Reading the Gospels, you don't get the impression that Jesus was stomping around, angry that we were making him do all this. You see that even though he was very aware of the pain he would need to endure, he enjoyed his time here with us.

> Reading the Gospels, you don't get the impression
> that Jesus was stomping around, angry that we were
> making him do all this.

He walked around making the world look more like what he created it to be. People's legs weren't intended to be crippled in God's plan, so he fixed people's legs and arms and skin and eyes. All along the way, Jesus left clues—some well hidden and others amazingly clear—as to who he really was.

Consider this example of a typical thing Jesus did. When anyone who was considered culturally unclean was about to cross paths or even come close to crossing paths with someone who was clean, he was required to shout, "Unclean!" in a loud voice. It might be that the person had any of a number of skin conditions referred to as leprosy, or perhaps he had a deformity. Whatever the issue, declaring his problem was humiliating and completely alienating from the rest of society.

In some towns, if an unclean person failed to follow this process, he could be stoned to death. But when God created the world he didn't intend that some people would be considered less valuable, less touchable. So God the Son went up to the most untouchable people and touched them. And when he did this, we got to see something amazing. Their infection didn't spread to Jesus; instead, his purity spread to them and simply pushed the disease they were suffering out of them.

**God the Son went up to the most untouchable people
and touched them.**

Jesus dealt with more than physical disease. He spent a great
deal of time working on people's hearts. He challenged the
rich to be aware of their weaknesses and the weak to see their
strengths. He walked through our world with us and showed us
how to live. He was exactly what you would expect God to be:
perfect.

God, Put to the Test

Let's skip to a very dark night when Jesus was around thirty-
three years old.

His human life was going to end soon, but not easily or quietly. Listen in as God the Son wrestles with what must come—
what an incredibly open God he is to show us this side of
himself:

> They went to the olive grove called Gethsemane, and
> Jesus said, "Sit here while I go and pray." He took Peter,
> James, and John with him, and he became deeply troubled
> and distressed. He told them, "My soul is crushed with
> grief to the point of death. Stay here and keep watch
> with me."

He went on a little farther and fell to the ground. He prayed that, if it were possible, the awful hour awaiting him might pass him by.

"Abba Father," he cried out, "everything is possible for you. Please take this cup of suffering away from me. Yet I want your will to be done, not mine." (Mark 14:32–36 NLT)

Wow.

Be careful here. The average person can read those sentences pretty fast. If we aren't mindful we will get through that chunk in a few seconds. One second Jesus is asking God if it is possible to avoid this; the next he's saying, "All right."

In Luke we get more of a feel for what that night was like for Jesus. Luke tells us he was sweating blood, which is an uncommon but real condition called *hematidrosis*. It happens when your body is put under extreme stress and tiny capillaries around your sweat glands burst and empty into your sweat ducts. Now Jesus was no wuss. He had directly faced down Satan, cast out demons, answered angry religious leaders, escaped raging mobs, and walked on water! He could handle pressure. Imagine the strain needed for that to happen!

As I said before, Jesus knew what was coming. He had made several references to this part of his role and what would be done with his physical body. He would be captured, beaten, flogged to near-death, and then crucified. It makes perfect sense that he would want to know from God the Father that this was all completely necessary. But he would do it all willingly. Jesus' enemies didn't capture him by surprise; they didn't somehow flush him out. He walked up to his captors and refused to use for his own benefit the miraculous power that he had so often used for the benefit of others. What was about to happen to him was equal parts terrible and necessary for us. And he knew it.

What was about to happen to him was equal parts terrible and necessary for us. And he knew it.

We really need to absorb this for a moment. You will see why soon.

In the account of Luke, we hear that Pilate handed him over to be flogged. Here is how that beating would typically go: First, your clothes would be stripped from your shoulders down to your buttocks. Then two Roman soldiers, called lictors, would take turns swinging a flagrum at your back and sides. A flagrum was made up of three to nine leather cords, up to several feet long, attached to a handle. The cords would be knotted and could be embedded with pieces of bronze and sheep bone. The most vicious would have a hook on the end called a *scorpion*. The intent was to remove large chunks of flesh and create crippling pain.

In fact, the scorpion wasn't used just to prepare victims for crucifixion. Its main use was as a device of torture to get information out of captives or criminals.[1]

The centurion in charge was responsible for stopping the flogging before the victim died. A third-century historian,

Eusebius of Caeasarea, said of these prisoners, "Their bodies were frightfully lacerated. Christian martyrs in Smyrna were so torn by the scourges that their veins were laid bare, and the inner muscles, sinews, even entrails, were exposed."[2] Oftentimes, after their backs were flogged, they would be flipped over and receive the same treatment on their stomachs.[3]

Jesus wouldn't just have been wounded by all this. His skin was literally ripped to shreds.

But the worst was still to come.

The actual crucifixion hadn't even begun yet. The word itself should let us know how bad things would get. *Crucifixion* is derived from the word *cruciare*, which means "to torture and torment." In fact, in the first-century BC, Cicero referred to it as "the most cruel and atrocious of punishments."[4]

In his article "A Physician Testifies About the Crucifixion," C. Truman Davis walks us through the crucifixion process:

Jesus [is] quickly thrown backward with His shoulders against the wood. The legionnaire feels for the depression at the front of the wrist. He drives a heavy, square, wrought-iron nail through the wrist and deep into the wood. Quickly, he moves to the other side and repeats the action, being careful not to pull the arms too tightly, but to allow some flexion and movement. The patibulum [crossbeam] is then lifted in place at the top of the stipes and the titulus reading "Jesus of Nazareth, King of the Jews" is nailed in place.

The left foot is now pressed backward against the

right foot, and with both feet extended, toes down, a nail is driven through the arch of each, leaving the knees moderately flexed. The Victim is now crucified. As He slowly sags down with more weight on the nails in the wrists, excruciating pain shoots along the fingers and up the arms to explode in the brain—the nails in the wrists are putting pressure on the median nerves. As He pushes Himself upward to avoid this stretching torment, He places His full weight on the nail through His feet. Again there is searing agony of the nail tearing through the nerves between the metatarsal bones of the feet.

...Hours of limitless pain, cycles of twisting, joint-rending cramps, intermittent partial asphyxiation, searing pain as tissue is torn from His lacerated back as He moves up and down against the rough timber. Then another agony begins...a terrible crushing pain deep in the chest as the pericardium slowly fills with serum and begins to compress the heart.

...It is now almost over. The loss of tissue fluids has reached a critical level; the compressed heart is struggling to pump heavy, thick, sluggish blood into the tissue; the tortured lungs are making a frantic effort to gasp in small gulps of air.[5]

It was terrible, and it took a long time to cause death. Jesus suffered for hours.

All that, for us. Sin was our problem, and God provided the solution. And the most amazing part of it all? He wasn't angry.

Not the least bit resentful. In Jesus' last moments, in what was undoubtedly thrashing pain, he looked at a criminal who was justifiably being crucified beside him and forgave him. He looked down at the people who were mocking him, even gambling for his clothes while he died, and forgave them as well.

Sin was our problem, and God provided the solution.

All that, because we needed it and he loves us. The apostle Paul, a guy who was once a persecutor of the people who followed Jesus, was led by God to say it like this: "God put his love on the line for us by offering his Son in sacrificial death while we were of no use whatever to him" (Romans 5:8 MSG).

In "The World's Last Night," C. S. Lewis wrote, "Christ died for men precisely because men are *not* worth dying for; to make them worth it."[6] While we were still rejecting him, God came down and died for us. Amazing.

What God's Past Performance Shows

Remember the infection we talked about earlier? Now, here is the truly amazing part: God's track record reveals that God the Father allowed Jesus' death to provide the antidote that we so desperately need, and that antidote, when we choose to apply it, eradicates the infection from our souls. The thing we are completely unable to do, God did. And with that infection gone, the quarantine is lifted and God, just like a parent who has been kept too long from his child, sweeps us up in his arms and we are reconnected to him.

All the way back in the Garden of Eden, we clearly heard from God what the boundaries were. We rejected them and brought on the consequences of our decision. God continued to reach out to us and love us. We rejected and forgot him. Remember now, this is God, not a stranger on the street; he deserves better. Then Jesus, God the Son, came on the scene and lived and showed us how to live and suffered that horrible death so we could have an antidote for the infection we released in the first place.

If you ask me, that shows an awful lot of love. God's past behavior shows that he has treated us much better than we have deserved.

God's past behavior shows that he has treated us much better than we have deserved.

But it gets even better.

After my freshman year at Virginia Tech, I accepted a summer job that offered the opportunity to travel, lots of money, fun people to work with, and a great boss—me. I sold books door-to-door in California. I hated it like death and I eventually concocted a ridiculous plan to quit.

Suffice it to say that I made no money whatsoever from that job. The reason was simple. I made money only if I made sales, and I didn't make very many. I learned the joys of being paid on commission: you sell it, and you get to keep a portion of the profits for yourself. Anyone who has been a waiter or waitress or sold cars, carpet, or even cell phones knows what I am talking about.

It makes so much sense: if you don't produce, you don't earn. It's a great motivator if you want to make sure that those who work for you *really* work for you. Your work determines your reward. A friend of mine just returned from Europe. She told me that in France the waiters and waitresses were typically slow, rude, and unconcerned with whether or not you were getting and enjoying your food. In Rome, it was quite the opposite. Guess which ones were paid with tips and which ones weren't?

And how many industries give merit-based bonuses? I think you see where I am going. The converse is also true, isn't it? If your reward is locked in, your reason for working hard is diminished.

Now, had God's goal been different, to sort of "put us on commission" would have been the way to go, wouldn't it? If God's goal had been to get us to do lots of "God-stuff," then he could have dangled the hope in front of us that maybe, just maybe we could someday earn the antidote we needed. Maybe someday we could be cured, if we played our cards right; if we did enough good deeds, read enough chapters of the Bible each day, prayed long enough. If we kept doing our part, he would keep doing his.

And he has a pretty good reward lined up, doesn't he?

"Look, God's home is now among his people! He will live with them, and they will be his people. God himself will be with them. He will wipe every tear from their eyes, and there will be no more death or sorrow or crying or pain. All things are gone forever." And the one sitting on the throne said, "Look, I am making everything new! ...Write this down, for what I tell you is trustworthy and true." (Revelation 21:3–5 NLT)

The world, fixed. Everything from my shoulder not popping out of the socket when I fall on it to no more cancer. Child abuse and school shootings—all of it, gone.

So, God has something for us, and had his goal been different, then Christianity wouldn't be all that different from most other world religions: You would get what you earned. You would live well, and at death, you would hope for the best. A good prize will do wonders.

The Right Reward

When I was in high school, a popular radio station threw a contest, and it was pretty simple. You had to take a regular size index card and write the phrase "I love K-92 FM" on it. Whichever school had sent in the most cards at the end of the contest would be declared the winner. The winning school would get a free live concert from the Jets. (Anyone who was—and in my case, still is—into eighties cheese rock would know the Jets.)

Within two weeks you couldn't find index cards at a store within two hours of us.

On weekends, groups of students would road-trip three or four hours to get to places that had the index cards we needed. Those students would arrive back at the school to a welcome more enthusiastic than the drivers of the sled-dog teams received when bringing the first antibiotic shipments of the spring to northern Alaska settlers. I remember writing "I love K-92 FM" until my hand went numb. Then I would switch hands until the circulation came back and I was off again. I don't remember how many cards were sent in, but it was neck and neck between us and our crosstown rival high school. And they won.

I do remember being very excited to hear that the Jets lip-synched the whole concert, which consisted of two songs! But that bit of vengeance isn't my point.

The right reward can really motivate. Imagine, high school-ers who probably complained anytime they were asked by their parents to do household chores (I know I did) were willing to write themselves into early carpal tunnel syndrome for a lip-synched concert of two songs.

But whether it's index cards for high schoolers or a fixed world and cured souls for the rest of us, the right reward can do a lot.

But God blew it.

God's "Mistake"

God had the chance to make us sweat it out. To hold out on us about whether or not we would make it "in" until we died. He could have gotten much more "God-stuff" out of us. We could have lived the way our kids spend the week before Christmas: being supernice, vying for everything they put on their lists. But God shot that chance. He makes it powerfully clear that our spiritual destiny is beyond our ability to affect through our own efforts. It isn't a question of doing enough "God-stuff" to be cured of the infection. The infection is everywhere and constantly being reproduced in our souls. God tells us how we can access the cure and then how we can be sure that we will be with him forever.

He could have gotten much more "God-stuff" out of us.

Jesus says this in the account of his life recorded by his follower and good friend John: "Don't let your hearts be troubled. Trust in God, and trust also in me.... Jesus told him, 'I am the way, the truth, and the life. No one can come to the Father except through me" (John 14:1, 6 NLT). Want more? "My sheep listen to my voice; I know them, and they follow me. I give them eternal life, and they will never perish.... The Father and I are one" (John 10:27–30 NLT).

Paul says,

> God is so rich in mercy, and he loved us so much, that even though we were dead because of our sins, he gave us life.... God saved you by his grace when you believed. And you can't take credit for this; it is a gift from God. Salvation is not a reward for the good things we have done, so none of us can boast about it. For we are God's masterpiece. He has created us anew in Christ Jesus. (Ephesians 2:4–5, 8–10 NLT)

God's mistake in all this? He didn't dangle anything. Like a parent who has been kept from his children, God comes tearing back to us as soon as we accept his gift.

Like a parent who has been kept from his children, God comes tearing back to us as soon as we accept his gift.

He doesn't dangle eternity with himself in a fixed world in front of us any more than he twists our arms behind our backs with images of eternity in hell to scare us. He simply demonstrates the reality of both and allows us the means and the freedom to make that choice for ourselves. Just as in the Garden.

He has been clear. We won't and cannot earn the antidote

we need. Life with God isn't something we do certain things well enough to achieve. Even good things. God gives us the thing that we cannot get for ourselves, even though we are the cause of the problem. We benefit from his suffering and pain. That shows a whole lot of care for us.

To Answer Our Question

Ready for answers to the questions we asked at the start of the chapter: "Where was God that day?" "Where is he in all of our pain?" "Where was he in that horrible moment...?"

The same place he was when God the son, Jesus, was tortured and unfairly killed on that cross. God the Father was still in heaven, watching with the deepest form of anguish as his Son was killed. Unlike Mary, Jesus' mother, who could at least turn away for brief moments to hide her eyes from the terrible sight, God would have experienced it purely: no sleep to escape into, no distractions. Imagine that.

But remember, because of the nature of the Trinity, God was also on the cross. God the Son himself was physically suffering and enduring all we have talked about. God the Son experienced leaving heaven to come to earth—not exactly trading up. He submitted to living in a human body that got hungry and sick, and he faced every kind of difficulty. Finally, the culmination of his earthly ministry and all that service brought him to the cross, where he suffered and gave his life.

> **God the Son experienced leaving heaven to come to earth—not exactly trading up.**

God the Holy Spirit needed to restrain himself—from just reaching and pulling Jesus right off the cross and ending the whole thing, from using the power at his disposal to prevent this unfair act. Three days later we are told the Holy Spirit was finally able to use that power and raised Jesus' body back to life.

I bet God's grief was the same on your particular days of suffering as he saw the evil in this world harm people for whom he has shown so much love. God can relate to the pain of those who lost loved ones because he has lost loved ones. God can relate to the pain of those injured because he has been injured. And God can relate to those whose pain is that they were simply unable to stop what was happening—whether they were in the buildings but didn't know what to do, or because they were across the country—because he has been forced to watch the unthinkable happen. He was able to end it and yet knew that, at that moment, he could not.

> **God can relate to the pain of those who lost loved ones because he has lost loved ones.**

In those horrible moments on that now-infamous day, God was simultaneously feeling the pain of those parents as the grim reality was settling in that this summer break wouldn't be at all as they had planned, the horror of the rest of us who watched everything from around the corner or around the world as this new reality settled into our lives, and the fear and pain of those physically wounded or killed.

"We don't have a priest [Jesus] who is out of touch with our reality. He's been through weakness and testing, experienced it all—all but the sin" (Hebrews 4:15 MSG). Simply put, Jesus gets us. He gets what we are going through. Because he has been through it on every angle.

We have a God who grieves with us but also understands the stakes.

We have a God who grieves with us but also understands the stakes.

But why not just hurry up and get to the point where you do fix it, God? Peter, another apprentice and friend of Jesus, answered complaints about this very issue: "The Lord isn't really being slow...as some people think. No, he is being patient for your sake. He does not want anyone to be destroyed, but wants everyone to repent" (2 Peter 3:9 NLT).

The Bottom Line

God can, and will, fix the world. But for the world to be fixed, the evil in it must be obliterated. If you haven't ever accepted the antidote, quite simply part of the reason he waits is for you. For those of us who have, he calls us to be agents of good in a world ripped apart by evil. Virginia Tech will not be the last place this type of violence occurs, and we won't be the last people harmed. So our lives are to be spent serving and helping those around us, and reminding them that everything we are experiencing, God has experienced.

Paul puts it very simply, but his words resound with challenge: "Don't let evil conquer you, but conquer evil by doing good" (Romans 12:21 NIV).

Until God deals with that evil permanently, at least we know he is in this mess with us and is being fair. He hasn't walled himself off from us or the consequences of being connected with us.

At least we know he plays by his own rules.

Questions for Reflection and Discussion

1. Do you notice the balance of justice and tenderness that God showed Adam and Eve in the Garden after their disobedience was uncovered?

2. As you have read the Gospels (Matthew, Mark, Luke, and John), have you noticed how Jesus didn't seem angry to be here? His earthly life was so much harder and his death so much more painful because of our rebellion—but you don't see him stomping around the way we might were we in his position. Remembering that Jesus is God the Son,

what does that make you think about God's love for us? What does that reveal about him?

3. Have you ever taken the time to really reflect on how torturous Jesus' flogging and execution were?

4. Look at how God set up the good news that we could be reconnected with him. He took the bulk of the pain and effort upon himself and gives us the opportunity through all that pain and sacrifice to walk into this new relationship with him. What parts of that reconciliation are you most grateful you don't have to do?

5. When you reflect on the shootings of April 16, the deaths on September 11, or whatever day seems the darkest to you, can you understand how deeply God suffered on those days as well?

9

Okay, but Is He Good?

You have your reasons for reading this book. We have talked about how we can all struggle with the idea that God seems to be managing the world pretty poorly. Or we have at least wished human lives didn't have so much pain and suffering. And we have seen the suffering in high-definition: We have friends who have lost jobs or not even been able to get one—or we have lost jobs ourselves. We have seen family members or friends struggle under the weight of debilitating illnesses or injuries—or we struggle with them ourselves. We see the impact of chronic poverty on others or feel it personally.

If any of us were asked to take out a sheet of paper and write twenty names of people who are suffering right now in ways we think they shouldn't have to, it wouldn't take long to make that list.

If you are interacting with the question of whether or not God should be fired, there is a very specific reason for it. Let's look at some.

Why Are You Reading This Book?

Some people bought this book because they are enduring terrible things and really want to know what God could be thinking. Others who bought this book have not personally suffered much, but they are quite curious about what a follower of Jesus would say in God's defense. People in both of these groups may be very close to making the decision to fire God.

As someone who had to grapple deeply with issues of faith and suffering prior to becoming a follower of Jesus (and throughout the duration of my following him), I understand some of what both types of readers are going through. I remember people telling me how *right* it was for me to become a follower of Jesus. As I mentioned earlier, I researched heavily the historical claims about Jesus Christ: the accuracy of the ancient texts, prophecy that could be dated to hundreds of years prior to when those prophecies came true. Over time it became very clear that there was a lot of evidence for the *rightness* of this.

After a while, believing that all the objective evidence was coincidental seemed to take more faith than saying, "There is a God who is real and who did this." Sure, the Bible has some wild stuff in it, but if so much that can be researched proves itself to be true, that makes a strong argument for what cannot be checked.

The Bible has some wild stuff in it.

So, if you are like me, you can say that God is real and fair in how he looks at us. But there's another question that is just as important: is he good? We don't just want a God who is just; we also want one who is good. I want to know that the poor kids in our children's classrooms matter even more to God than they do to me. That he takes note of the yelling we can sometimes hear from the apartments behind our house. That he notices the sadness that poor kids in our area feel when they come back to school the first day after Christmas in the same clothes they had before and are forced to look at the veritable catalogs walking all around them. We need to know that this next Thanksgiving he is comforting families of the shooting survivors. We need to know he is close to families torn apart by cancer. We need to know he is bothered by the desperate conditions affecting so much of the continent of Africa.

We don't just want a God who is just; we also want one who is good.

You might be reading this in an effort to get a grasp on God's concern for the messed-up world we live in. For others, it is personal. You have been dropped to the ground by the suffering you have had forced on you. Maybe your suffering feels something like the way J. R. Woodward described it:

Just imagine you are surfing a wave and you get thrown underwater. You weren't expecting it so you don't have a chance to take a breath; all of a sudden you just cannot breathe. You are tumbling at the bottom getting banged up and trying to get yourself oriented so you can come up for air. Wave after wave hits you and right when you think you can surface and fill your lungs with life again—even just get a break from the hurt—another wave spins you under and tosses you to the bottom again. All the while you are going through this you are aware that everyone around you is enjoying a wonderful day in the sun.

Is Suffering What We Deserve?

Given how far-reaching and normal these questions are, it should come as no surprise that people asked them of Jesus. In Jesus' time, there was a strong belief that God essentially gave you what you deserved.

In Jesus' time, there was a strong belief that God essentially gave you what you deserved.

In Job, what is commonly thought to be the oldest book in the Scriptures, we see this perception played out.

Job was a very devout man. After an odd debate between God and Satan, Satan was given the authority to bring huge amounts of suffering to Job. Essentially, in one day, Job lost his living, his home, even his children. To top it all off, he ended up with nasty and painful boils covering his body. In Job chapter 2 we catch up to him sitting by a fire in mourning clothes, scraping his boils with a piece of broken pottery. His wife even adds the final blow when she, in her own anger and sadness, tells Job to "curse God and die!" (verse 8 NIV).

But help is on the way. Job's buddies have heard of his problems and are coming to comfort their friend. And they are remarkable at it. The first thing they do is sit with him without saying a word for seven days! That is support.

Day eight, they adjust their strategy.

Eliphaz suggests that Job must have done something to earn what he is getting. In his view of God, admittedly very primitive, you get what you deserve. For this caliber of suffering to fall on his friend, something bad must have been going on in Job's world. Eliphaz seemed to genuinely care for his friend. He was just trying to get him to admit his failures. The only problem was that Job couldn't figure out what he had done to cause all the pain and loss.

Then Bildad jumps in. Bildad suggests it was the wrongdoing of Job's children that brought disaster on him. In Bildad's worldview, the lightning strikes pretty close to the infraction. You see in the B.C. comic strip the misadventures of several prehistoric people. Someone does something wrong and then there's a massive ZOT! And the wrongdoer is toast. Bildad was trying to help his friend see that Job's kids had gotten out of hand, so God took care of it. Done and done.

The final friend, Zophar, even goes so far as to hope that

God will soon start to go after Job for his insistence that he didn't do anything to bring this on himself.

All these guys seemed to care for Job in his deep suffering—remember, they sat with their friend in silence for *seven* days! The only problem was that they were wrong.

Finally, God does speak. He challenges many of Job's anguished words, but he never once says that Job's friends were right. He makes it clear that Job didn't deserve what happened—only that there was much more going on than Job could possibly understand.

The viewpoint that Eliphaz, Bildad, and Zophar held had entrenched itself in the Jewish understanding of God and was alive and well in Jesus' day. Jews were well versed in their history—remarkably so. They had heard the accounts about how when the people of Israel turned away from God, he sent prophets to warn them: "Israel, you have turned away from me. Come back."

Almost inevitably they didn't. And just as inevitably, God would either send difficulty on them to get their attention or simply remove his protection. They would get the idea and turn back to him and he would reestablish his connection with them. This occurred again and again over hundreds of years.

The Heart Connection

But over that time, the Jews seemed to have missed that God's protection wasn't just about what they did; it was also about the status of their hearts. Jesus takes the religious leaders to task in the biography written by Luke the physician: "Woe to you Pharisees, because you give God a tenth of your mint, rue and all other kinds of garden herbs, but you neglect justice and the love of God. You should have practiced the latter without leaving the former undone" (Luke 11:42 NIV).

The religious leaders in that day were being careful to give the temple a tenth of everything they received—even a tenth of the produce they grew. That is dedication! But they had gotten caught up in the rules, and likely in the public acclaim that type of giving brought. They were the religious rock stars; the dedication was impressive but had become about the Pharisees themselves.

Remember, Jesus made clear that what they were doing was good. Giving has always been a way for God's people to show their faith in him. But Jesus wanted them to give their hearts rather than just their herbs and funds. Unfortunately, that never happened. The Pharisees became obsessed with doing the right thing without any sense of why. They missed the point. God didn't want them to just obey. Sure, their obedience was important as a gesture of trust and honor, and as a means of protection. But the stuff they did *for* God should have been the by-product of hearts *given to* God.

**The stuff they did *for* God should have been the
by-product of hearts given *to* God.**

They turned God into a taskmaster instead of a loving father. And it went downhill from there.

Jesus' Response to Innocent Deaths

Jesus was confronted with that taskmaster perspective. Luke recorded that in the area now known as Silwan—or Siloam, as it was called in Jesus' day—two horrible things had recently happened. The first involved Pontius Pilate. Pilate was the procurator of the province of Judea once the Romans took control. Think of him as part sheriff, part judge, and part general. He had quite a bit of power, but that power was strongly controlled by Herod's whim. And as the king of Judah, Herod had a lot of whims.

Pilate had recently ordered soldiers to cruelly murder several Galileans as they were offering their sacrifices. The surprise attack occurred in the temple. This kind of killing simply wasn't done. Beyond the horror of the killings was the realization that the people were murdered in a place designed for the worship of God, not the anger of men.

When Jesus hears the news of this tragedy, he brings up another: "And what about the eighteen people who died when the tower in Siloam fell on them? Were they the worst sinners in Jerusalem? No" (Luke 13:4–5 NLT).

So we have two different but terrible circumstances. In the one, we have a wrong that was planned and carried out against people. This wasn't a natural phenomenon; it wasn't a freak accident. The people who did the killing meant to do the killing, and those killed didn't want it to happen. In the other instance, barring some sort of plan to cause the toppling of the tower, it was an accident. Probably no one intended it; no one thing caused it. It was a relatively common occurrence in Jesus' day, having towers topple over. Two very different scenarios were linked by the fact that they caused multiple deaths.

Jesus asks the same strange question of both situations to directly challenge the Jewish belief that people's difficulty is caused by their wrong: "Do you think those Galileans were worse sinners than all the other people from Galilee?" (Luke 13:2 NIV). And then again, "Were they [the people who died when the tower fell] the worst sinners in Jerusalem?" (verse 4 NIV). His intent and his answer couldn't be clearer.

The Galileans, regardless of the individual lives they had led, didn't earn those deaths. Remember, these would have been normal people who had probably done plenty of wrong things. Regardless of the fact that they had committed different levels of wrong in their lives, these people didn't deserve the deaths they suffered. Those deaths were not an indication that God was against them, that God was cruel. These people died because of an evil king and poor construction.

Once and for All: Why?

We would do well to realize what is missing in this. Here, Jesus has the opportunity to put the questions to rest once and for all: "Why? Why would God allow this to happen? Why wouldn't he stop it, hold the building up, stop the soldiers? He could, right?"

As we get into this, let's remember that by this point Jesus had often revealed the power he had access to: miraculous healings on many occasions, provision of food where there was none, power over storms. He even made death go away a few times.

When Jesus had just been told about the temple deaths he said another strange thing. He told the people that, among other things, they should turn to God or they would die as well: "Unless you repent, you too will all perish" (Luke 13:5 NIV). He even repeated himself! This from a man who showed incredible compassion! Paul said it this way in his letter to the church in Philippi:

> Though he [Jesus] was God, he did not think of equality with God as something to cling to. Instead, he gave up his divine privileges; he took the humble position of a slave and was born as a human being. When he appeared in human form, he humbled himself in obedience to God and died a criminal's death on a cross. (Philippians 2:6–8 NLT)

The level of concern Jesus' coming to earth demonstrates for us is breathtaking. Someone like that wouldn't be crass or uncaring. He loved everybody! He demonstrated care and concern for even those who didn't at all deserve or ask for it. So his response to the questions surrounding those deaths is very odd.

The level of concern Jesus' coming to earth demonstrates for us is breathtaking.

Or maybe not. If someone *that* loving says something *that* strong to you, you should pause and ask yourself why. Jesus was actually dealing with something very similar to what we face today, just with a different application.

Remember—in Jesus' day, the general idea was that you got what you deserved. If you were killed unfairly when you were offering sacrifices to God, you really weren't killed unfairly. God was paying you back for something. That was why Jesus took this awful news and turned it into a warning not to lose sight of the main issue. And the main issue was not what those poor men did to deserve to be cut down like that. The main issue was *the status of the hearts of the people around Jesus that day*. That was why Jesus brought up the tower. People were asking why God singled out the Galileans to be killed. Jesus was saying God didn't.

Here we begin to have a lot in common with some people who lived almost two thousand years ago. The people in the crowd that day, like us, were trying to figure Jesus out. Some were already followers, but others were deciding if they would be. And as they wandered around with Jesus, they dragged their cultural baggage behind them. For the Jews it was a "You get what you deserve" mentality; for us it is a "If God were loving and strong enough, he would stop more of this suffering" mentality.

Is God being wrongly accused? Jesus' point that day was actually twofold. First, he was telling the people around him to be careful with "You get what you deserve" thinking. But he was also reminding them, and us now, that we must not allow our cultural baggage to suppress the main issue. He said, "Don't miss the point. Turn to God. Realize that you must reconcile, and don't let that idea get away from you in the fog of your questions about undue suffering."

Is God being wrongly accused?

Recognize here what Jesus wasn't saying. He wasn't saying their questions didn't matter. On numerous occasions Jesus took time and great pains to answer the concerns and questions of those around him. But he also made sure that those around him kept the main things the main things. He corrected wrong thinking and then reminded them that it wasn't the questioning of what God was doing that mattered the most. It was the finding and turning to God that mattered most.

Jesus was calling people to not get lost in details that, even though they mattered (those killed were real people)—those details weren't the most important things. It wasn't enough to just wonder and then wander off confused. At some point, conclusions were called for.

Jesus' point that day is cogent to our discussion today. The people around Jesus were in danger of missing the most important issue facing their fragile lives—which was to understand the fragility of their lives. The point wasn't to understand every aspect of why things happened. As much as we want that, we aren't offered it. As much as we want to believe that people get what they deserve (until it pertains to us), many times they don't. We want a sense of predictability for our future. If not an ironclad guarantee, then at least strong likelihoods.

But Jesus was showing something different. He was calling on them, in light of how the world was working then, to turn back to God. Jesus was saying the horror in life should actually bring us closer to God, not push us farther away.

The horror in life should actually bring us closer to God, not push us farther away.

C. S. Lewis said that discovering the Christ of Christianity is like finding "a religion you couldn't have guessed."[1] In his novel *The Lion, the Witch and the Wardrobe*, Mr. Beaver was asked if the character that represented Jesus in the allegory, the great Aslan, was safe. He replied, "Safe?...Who said anything about safe? 'Course he isn't safe. But he's good. He's the King, I tell you."[2]

A passage written by one of Jesus' closest friends during his time here on earth, John, describes the heart of God very well: "He will wipe every tear from their eyes. There will be no more death or mourning or crying or pain, for the old order of things has passed away" (Revelation 21:4 NIV).

The verse from Revelation answers the questions: Is he good? Does he care?

He came to earth and suffered and died for us, and one day, our suffering will be over. One day neither Jesus nor we will have to cry at any more friends' gravesites.

And in the meantime, he shows his concern for our planet by calling on us to be his emissaries in correcting its wrongs. In short, we get to trade clear death and separation for true life and connection.

Maybe now we can acknowledge that we have been too hard on God. That perhaps we have been unaware of issues that God must be aware of. So now, how about taking a look at how we find him?

Questions for Reflection and Discussion

1. What makes a book like this interesting for you? Why?

2. How convinced are you that God is truly good, loving, and aware of you and your situation right now? Has that changed at all as a result of reading this book so far?

3. If you were sitting with Job and his friends, do you think you would tend to agree with them? Or if you arrived on the scene a few thousand years later, in the day of the Pharisees, would you have agreed with their belief that people basically get what they deserve from God? How has your life demonstrated this belief?

4. What possible reason would Jesus have for his seemingly unsympathetic response to hearing about the men killed by Pilate's soldiers while they were worshiping?

5. What is the point Jesus is trying to make with his statement: "Unless you repent, you too will all perish" (Luke 13:3 NIV)?

6. How does Jesus' warning—to keep the central things central—apply to us today?

7. What issues in our world obscure the fact that we are disconnected from the God who created us, the God who desperately wants to provide us the antidote for our infection and then be in relationship with us from then on?

8. What do you think Jesus would say to *you* if he were physically alive today and you had brought him similar news to the words recorded in Luke 13?

PART III

Searching for the Good God

10

A Look at Our Searching

With our second son, Seth, we have a very regular experience. The following occurs about 4.5 seconds before we have to go out the door to get our children to school: *"Mom! Dad!* [He shouts at about 100 decibels.] I can't find my shoes/ homework/ permission slip/ book bag/ lunch/ left thumb."

In our calmest voices, my wife or I will then share valuable instructive guidance: *"What? Again?!* This is why we tell you to put away your shoes when you take them off at night! I mean, we just *had* this exact conversation yesterday! Remember? You said you would never misplace your shoes/homework/permission slip/ book bag/lunch...again! *Remember?!"*

We then have him start to look for whatever it is he lost, and as we are getting our keys (when *we* can find those right away) and our coats, something remarkable happens. It is one of the most infuriating and amazing things he can do and regularly does. Seth proceeds to *not* look for the missing item. Sure, he says he is, probably even believes he is. If you call downstairs to him, he is furiously checking everywhere. But many times I have snuck down the steps only to find him watching a TV that happens to be on. Even watching commercials! In his developing, delightful mind, the fact that he and we are aware that there is a problem seems to be enough.

Just knowing you need to look for something, or even starting the search, isn't the same thing as finding what you are looking for, no more than realizing a tornado is coming at you makes you safe. The awareness that something that strong is headed toward you is only the first step—then you must seek cover. Realizing that something needs to be done just isn't the same thing as doing it, and realizing that something is missing is different from finding it.

Seeking vs. Finding

It isn't enough only to seek and question; it wasn't in Jesus' day, and it isn't now. Please understand: I am not saying that in your searching, questioning God about your concerns isn't valuable. It clearly is. Prior to becoming a follower of Jesus, and even to this day, I remain a questioner of God. God has always been able to handle my questions and concerns. But we need to admit that we can get lost in them. When I talk with many of my friends who do not follow Jesus, I feel that many think seeking is enough.

I remain a questioner of God.

When my son Seth goes to school, it isn't enough for him to tell Ms. Williams that he looked for his homework paper. He needs to have found it. In many ways, God is the same way. I understand seeking is easier said than done. We are, unfortunately, much better lookers than finders. In *Subversive Spirituality*, Eugene Peterson describes our plight this way:

> Spirituality, a fusion of intimacy and transcendence, overnight becomes a passion for millions of North Americans. It should be no surprise that a people so badly trained in intimacy and transcendence might not do too well in their quest. Most anything at hand that gives a feeling of closeness—whether genitals or cocaine—will do for intimacy. And most anything exotic that induces a sense of mystery—from mantras to river rafting—will do for transcendence.[1]

You and I, according to Peterson, are looking for something spiritually meaningful. He suggests, though, that we're not very skilled at actually finding anything definitive. Perhaps we would disagree with the strength of his statement, but he seems to have a point: We long for something we aren't well equipped to find. We are better seekers than finders.

Who Is Right?

When I was starting to search out spiritual things, it was daunting to say the least. I remember the feeling. Everyone suggested his or her way was right. Even if a particular religion or belief didn't claim there was only one way to know God, its followers said the religions that did were wrong! Some commentators from different perspectives say all or most perspectives are virtually the same, and then you have just as many practitioners of those perspectives saying how different they are!

So, to be fair, coming to spiritual conclusions isn't the easiest thing to do.

**Coming to spiritual conclusions isn't the easiest thing
to do.**

One thing I have noticed among my friends who would call themselves spiritual seekers and not spiritual finders is that they typically have a common concern. They don't want to be seen as narrow-minded, closed to any religious or philosophical school of thought beyond the one they ultimately accept. In our culture today, saying that you know what is true about religious issues makes you seem more like an extremist than anything else. This reality puts seekers in a very similar position to many of those around Jesus when he heard about the killings we spoke of in the last chapter.

My friends highly value freedom for people to come to their own conclusions about the world, including the role of God (or the lack thereof) in that world. I do too. The worst thing I can do as a follower of Jesus is try to force someone else to agree with my conclusions. I pray the days of arm-twisting, hell-based, guilt-laden conversions are past us. People need to be drawn to the chance to be forgiven for what they have done. But they must also be drawn to become a part of God's ongoing story that he is now writing with us. They need to see that it is through Christ that they can have the greatest impact on people's needs and have their own most central needs met as well.

But I fear my friends have taken it a step too far. And I fear this is where their error lies.

Today, it is culturally wrong to be sure about something because if you are, you are seen as closed-minded and controlling. A good friend of mine and an exciting church planter in Hollywood, J. R. Woodward, describes it this way in his excellent essay, "Is Conversion a Four-Letter Word?"

> It is easy for those who live under the meta-narrative of modernity to slip into the idea that the gospel is a set of objective facts for an individual to "believe" and a sinner's prayer for individuals to pray, instead of an invitation to "switch stories" allowing God's reality to re-shape them, so that they might partner with Him to bring more of heaven to earth.[2]

Many in our culture have come to a great conclusion: we want very much to avoid trampling someone else's beliefs. We want people to realize they matter because they are made by God, not just because they agree with us about him. But I fear at times we have gone too far, and, as a result, we miss opportunities for those we care about to hear of the amazing love of God.

So much of our cultural arrogance of the last century has finally been dispensed with, has finally been hung up. We are loath to declare that any one person is "right." And, in many ways, that is a good thing. As a culture, we are becoming better listeners, more willing to enter into the worlds of those around us instead of insisting they drop what they are doing to come into ours. My concern is that in this process some pretty good babies have been thrown out with the bathwater, so to speak. We have gone from a society known for thinking it is right too much of the time to one that is wary of anyone really ever thinking they are right at all.

Simply put, culturally, spiritual seeking is a great thing to do. Spiritual finding is not.

Specifics Matter

Once you are a spiritual finder, you become responsible to the specifics of what you have found. You are expected to not just live within the guidelines of those specifics, but at some level to communicate those specifics to others. You are placed in a position that could get tricky. If any of the beliefs you have accepted as truth indicate that their acceptance is important, you have to respond to that.

Very few of us want to be the guy who demands adherence to specific beliefs from others. We don't want to be the one who is always disagreeing with those around us. We are fighting cultural influences and fears that we will inexplicably become another annoying extremist. What if we are wrong? What if we come off as boorish or closed-minded? It is easier to just continue looking.

But it is more than that, isn't it? We can fear what will happen to us should we decide that we, too, would like to become followers of Jesus. We fear that slowly but surely we will develop a liking for three-piece polyester suits. We will start to carry around a Bible as big as our arm that could substitute for a barbell if necessary. We will begin to have that sneer whenever someone from the gay community walks by us; we will listen only to Christian music and allow our kids to play only with other "good Christian kids." We fear that we will end up feeling superior to "all those nonbelievers" around us. Following the Jesus who demands that kind of snobbery, though, doesn't seem to us to make his followers better at all; it seems to make them meaner. And we want none of that.

Following the Jesus who demands that kind of snobbery doesn't seem to us to make his followers better at all; it seems to make them meaner.

In Jesus' day, the belief in the idea that you get what you deserve was self-protective in nature. If bad things didn't really happen to good people and if you avoided what bad people did, bad things would stay away. Today, our bias against spiritual finding is self-protective as well. If we cannot say for sure what is true about the world around us, then we feel we can live and let live. Jesus tells us today, as he told the people of his day: don't let the cultural perspective you live within keep you from the decisions that are most important to your soul. Again, seeking is not the same thing as finding.

The Ways We Search

There are many other reasons you may not decide to follow Jesus definitively. Let's take a look at what might be behind your spiritual seeking.

Most but not all of those who would consider themselves spiritual seekers, as opposed to finders, arrive at that destination by default: either they are convinced that any real clarity in the spiritual realm is unlikely, or they are convinced it's just too difficult to arrive at any clarity. Deep down, those seem to be the two most prevalent reasons.

But when I ask people to tell me how they are going to carry out the spiritual search, I rarely hear a plan. I rarely hear how they intend to try to distinguish between the tenets of different belief systems, or how they will try to live them out for a while to see for themselves, or if perhaps they might look into the evidence for the accuracy of different religious texts. Rarely do I hear a coherent strategy.

Seems we hope that we will figure it out as we go along.

We grab some great quotes, and there are a lot of them. Great books, essays, song lyrics, and poetry—all of us have been captured by powerful words that can shape us. Probably no one in the United States could have missed the amazing symbolism of Barack Obama taking his oath of office just across the mall from where Martin Luther King Jr. made his famous "I Have a Dream" speech—the speech that paved the way for Obama to stand there. Great words have made great differences.

When I ask people how they have developed their spiritual perspective, they tend to give me a list of powerful words or experiences they have had or witnessed. The more questions I ask about how they view God, the more I see a mosaic, and typically the image of God/god or goddess they have developed was born from an internal sense they have about what that God/god or goddess would or wouldn't look like. They accept the aspects of God that connect with their own internal moral compasses but reject those they don't agree with.

They accept the aspects of God that connect with their own internal moral compasses but reject those they don't agree with.

This approach makes perfect sense. Many of the people I interact with the most would fall into a new sociological category outlined in Paul Ray and Sherry Anderson's book, *The Cultural Creatives: How 50 Million People Are Changing the World*. The term "cultural creatives" describes a group of people spanning several age levels who share a common set of concerns. They tend to be more artistic, more interested in environmental and social justice causes, and more optimistic about the future and the impact they can have on it. They tend to be more educated and typically (but not always) pretty frustrated with both the political right and left.[3]

I consider myself one of them. And one of the things that I share with many is my cynicism.

A Hindrance to True Searching

I have shared several times that I am a recovering cynic. Perhaps I should reconsider that description because my goal isn't to fully leave my cynicism behind. In some ways I like it. At times, I feel it is necessary. Cultural creatives have seen staggering amounts of duplicity in our lives. We have seen a president parse the meaning of "is"; we have seen CEO after CEO cheat the workers who created the products that made their golden parachutes possible and then leave those same workers stranded. We have seen conservative religious leaders fail to be forthcoming about their own struggles as they condemn ours. Teachers are having sex with students, and students are shooting teachers. Even our parents are letting us down. What is left is very little ambient trust in anyone we don't know well. *Merriam-Webster's* definition of *cynic* would seem to apply well: "one who believes that human conduct is motivated wholly by self-interest."[4]

The word *cynic* itself has some interesting history behind it. It originally comes from the Greek word for "dog" or *kunikos*. It is possibly connected to the word *ku-n* (meaning "dog"), which was given to Diogenes of Sinope, who could be seen barking in public, urinating, or even committing lewd acts in the street. His philosophical sect, called *cynics*, believed that virtue was the only good in the world and that self-control was the only means of achieving that virtue. What his antics were showing, was that he held a deep contempt for the people around him. His bizarre actions were just how he chose to demonstrate it.[5] Most of us would not align with much of what the philosophical cynics hold to, and hopefully most of us aren't serial street-urinators, but we might have more in common with Diogenes than we think—and my processing of tragedy has shown me something.

I disagree with much of Diogenes' thinking in so many ways, and I would never take things to the level that he did. But some of my differences are more matters of degree than anything else. I could demonstrate the same level of contempt, and things like shootings and tsunamis and planes turned missiles would only make that contempt worse. Sure, for a while things get better, we love each other more, make more eye contact, and rally around one another. But over time we separate again, only this time we separate having looked deeply into just how much we can be hurt. Our vulnerability frightens us, so we try to protect ourselves from it.

Cynicism at its base is a self-protective act. The more we think pessimistically, the more we can somehow prepare for the inevitable letdowns. The more we can be sarcastic and caustic with people, the more we can keep a protective zone around ourselves. We aren't sucked in by anyone because we are rarely close to anyone.

Cynicism at its base is a self-protective act.

My point here is that when we, like Diogenes, demonstrate certain contempt for those around us, we end up looking for the worst in them. We especially like the failings that people have attempted to hide. After a while, you expect to find them. The people around you are guilty before any proof comes in.

Those of us who would call ourselves present, past, or reforming cynics all got there differently. Perhaps our parents let us down so often and so significantly that we found ourselves expecting to be let down by others. Maybe we experienced something in high school that shook our trust in those around us. Maybe we trusted too many people too easily, were hurt by that trust, and we decided never to trust again.

You take that preexisting condition of general mistrust and add tragedy to it, and you come up with a hardened cynic.

Cynicism, among other things, has led us to do something that is necessary in many ways but for which we aren't necessarily well equipped: Simply put, when spiritually seeking we go with our guts. But our guts may not always serve us as well as we might wish or think.

A God Who Looks a Lot Like Us

So we enter the discussion of God with a lot already figured out, whether or not we realize it. We cannot trust those who speak the loudest; we assume most people will not really be trustworthy in this pursuit—the church likely least of all. So we find ourselves on our own. It is no wonder that the gods we find look a lot like us.

What this process also belies is that we come to the search believing that the finding is less important than the searching. Our spiritual pursuit is more about our own personal and spiritual/emotional development and healing than an actual attempt to find anything that is discoverable and real.

Christian Smith, in his survey of three thousand American adolescents from many different faith traditions, asked questions about their beliefs and received this response: "Many adolescents responded with a shrug and 'whatever.'" Through their analysis of the survey results, Smith and his team introduced the term "moralistic therapeutic deism," which consists of beliefs like these:

1. A god exists who created and ordered the world and watches over human life on earth.

2. God wants people to be good, nice, and fair to each other, as taught in the Bible and by most world religions.

3. The central goal of life is to be happy and to feel good about oneself.

4. God does not need to be particularly involved in one's life except when God is needed to resolve a problem.

5. Good people go to heaven when they die.[6]

I know many people who would strongly connect with that description of God. That picture of God makes sense to us.

So we come to the spiritual search feeling as though we aren't likely to get a lot figured out; consequently we are left with a God who looks a lot like us, who makes sense to us, and who asks little of us.

But what we lose is the opportunity to interact with, walk with, and even reconnect with a transcendently powerful and loving God who asks much of us but gives back even more. We essentially look for a God who is much smaller, less loving, less interesting, and less good.

What we lose by looking only for a God who looks like us and makes sense to us is the great adventure of reconnecting with a God who (as Mr. Beaver said in C. S. Lewis's novel) isn't at all safe, but is thoroughly good. A God too big for us to create by our own devices, and too different from what we would expect to be easily found. A God who has been terribly represented by many who pick up microphones and claim to speak for him. A God who is not at all what we expect. But is better.

Questions for Reflection and Discussion

1. Do you agree or disagree that our culture values the search for, rather than the actual finding and living of, spiritual meaning and truth? Why or why not?

2. Eugene Peterson suggests that we are poorly equipped to handle the transcendent. Both because of this fact and as a result of it, we often settle for what is really not transcendent. Do you see yourself having settled for less than what is truly transcendent? In what way?

3. How can our desire to not trample someone else's belief system make it harder for us to discover or live out our personal belief system?

4. What have the Jesus followers around you done to make our culture at large feel that following Jesus is not a meaningful path to becoming more whole and spiritually connected with God? What have you done/could you do to reverse this?

5. How cynical are you? What are the implications of your cynicism? How does it impact your questions surrounding Jesus or your ability to follow him more closely?

6. In your everyday life, what factors impact whether you will give someone a fair hearing? Be honest. Which of

these factors are actually helpful and which should you potentially release? Why?

7. Would you consider yourself to be what Christian Smith and Melinda Lundquist Denton termed a "moral therapeutic deist"? Either way, would you say that any of the beliefs they list (shown on pages 207–208) describe how you view God or God's responsibility set? Do you feel that you have a sense of what the Scriptures say about these beliefs? What would that be?

11

Praise Whatever, Whenever

MAY I TELL YOU a terrible story?

To start with, Johnstown, Pennsylvania, was founded in 1794 primarily by German and Welsh immigrants. What started as a small outpost at the fork of the Conemaugh and Stoney Creek rivers grew into a town known for the quality of the steel from ore mined from its hills. In 1834, the town was awarded by being included on the Pennsylvania Maritime Canal system that was being dug to ultimately connect Philadelphia to Pittsburg. In the 1850s, the Cambria Iron Company and the Pennsylvania railroad came in. As the city continued to grow, it built out farther and eventually pushed onto the banks of the two rivers. This was not good because Johnstown was located at the fork of these two rivers, which created a floodplain.

As a part of the contract to have the canal run near it, the city was awarded money to build a dam. The townspeople needed the dam because the dry seasons in that part of the country would cause the river to run too low to be useful for a canal system. So the dam would be used to store water and allow it to be released as needed for the canals. In 1840, William Morris designed the South Fork Dam, and construction continued until 1852.

Considerable care went into the building of the South Fork Dam. The valley floor was cleared to the bedrock. The upstream portion of the embankment was built up in successive rolled layers of clay and earth that were two feet thick each. These were then "puddled" or allowed to sit underwater for two days to allow the air to dissolve out and make them watertight. The portions of the dam exposed to water were covered with shale and small stones called *riprap* so the action of the water working against the dam wouldn't weaken it. To add needed weight and strength to the embankment, the core consisted of shale, earth, and small stones, while the downstream section was built of mostly rocks, many in excess of ten tons.

Compared to other dams of its day, the South Fork Dam was massive. It stretched 918 feet across the valley and was more than 72 feet high. The earth and rock used was 10 feet thick at the top and in excess of 220 feet thick on the valley floor. Running under the center of the dam was a huge steel culvert system used to allow water to flow through the dam to the South Fork Creek River and then downstream to the canal system. In the event of heavy rains, an 85-foot-wide spillway was cut through solid rock on the eastern side.

In June 1852, the dam began to fill. Two small leaks were

found two years later and the dam was drained in order to fix them. In 1862, the culvert system section of the upstream part of the dam collapsed and a large section of the dam washed away. By this point the dam was considered too unsafe to fix again. As the canal system was outmoded by train transport, the dam was left to the river.

Eventually, in 1879 a wealthy business developer named Benjamin Ruff bought the dam and the five hundred surrounding acres, with the desire to construct an upscale summer resort. Later that year, a charter was written for the South Fork Hunting and Fishing Club.

Ruff began the process of fixing the dam. He hired a geological engineer with expertise in dam work and a plan was developed. When the engineer inspected the project, he saw that the past decision to not fix the dam was correct and the dam was indeed too dangerous to ever be fully operational. He reported his findings to Ruff.

He was fired.

Another man, one with expertise in the construction of railroad embankments, was brought in to supervise the rebuild. His plan was to essentially make a large embankment. It was much easier and less precise than the original construction, but one that seemed workable. One decision they made was to not redig the culvert system under the dam. It would have taken too long and cost too much, and they only needed the dam to hold the water, not send it on through to the old canal system. So it seemed sufficient.

As the repair progressed, there were several leaks, but they weren't large and they really couldn't be fixed as the dam could no longer be drained to get below the waterline.

In March 1881, the reconstruction of South Fork Dam was completed, the lake stocked, and the resort opened. And for eight years, the dam held fine. Granted, every now and then a leak would pop up, but nothing major happened. The resort brought a lot of money into the area, and even though lots of people joked the dam would break, no one really believed it would. People even built their houses right at the base of it. The dam was huge and obviously very strong. What could go wrong?

The fired engineer tried on several occasions to draw attention to the dam situation, but to no real avail. People thought it was just too big to break. After all, the dam was still massive and the area depended on the hunting club for needed revenues. Those two things, when combined, pushed away doubts and made important leaks seem unimportant.

Wonder why the lesson in dam rebuilding techniques? Hang in there. The answer is coming!

The Inevitable Happens

On May 28, 1889, a Nebraska rainstorm started traveling the roughly thousand miles east to Johnstown. When it arrived two days later, it was considered the worst downpour recorded in that section of the country. The U.S. Signal Service estimated that the storm dropped six to ten inches of rain in twenty-four hours.

Here is what made that very bad.

The lake behind the South Fork Dam already held twenty million tons of water. The repaired section of the dam was toward the middle, which bore the greatest amount of force. Because this section wasn't repaired well, it had settled about six inches and was the weakest part of the dam.

Every minute, four thousand cubic feet of water collected behind the dam. What wasn't seen as important when everything was going well was now precipitating a tragedy. That Nebraska storm didn't make something that was unbreakable break, it just demonstrated the already present weakness.

What wasn't seen as important when everything was going well was now precipitating a tragedy.

Simply put, it was just too much water.

John Clarke was the resident engineer for the South Fork Dam. He was one of the first to recognize "too much water" was on the verge of becoming a reality. He had sounded this alarm before. Several times, actually, but cloudless skies make it awfully hard to be overly concerned with too much rain.

He put together a group of day laborers to go onto the dam itself and try to widen the spillway to get rid of more water. When that didn't work, he got on a horse and frantically rode the thirteen miles to town, screaming at people to get to high ground because the dam was about to break.

Hundreds of people listened to the warnings and began to climb higher, but thousands did not. Conventional wisdom was just too strong. They felt they would be fine—they had to be.

By the time Clarke returned to the dam, the lake was rising at a rate of one inch every ten minutes. By noon the water was freely flowing over the top of the dam, leaving the top intact but eating away at the far side, loosening rocks, trees, and everything else.

At 3:10 p.m., as one witness described, the entire repaired section "simply washed away."

The water rushed through this now-gigantic hole, and the entire twenty million tons of water emptied in forty-five minutes. A wall of water headed downstream at close to three stories high and almost sixty miles an hour. Huge Pennsylvania Railroad cars were swept up in the floodwall as if they were toys. More than two thousand people were killed and entire towns disappeared in five minutes.[1]

My point is this: just because the common view was that the dam was too strong to break didn't mean it in fact was. Sometimes the common view deserves reconsideration.

Sometimes the common view deserves reconsideration.

The Fear of Losing

In their book *Sway: The Irresistible Pull of Irrational Behavior*, Ori and Rom Brafman cite the amazing "twenty-dollar auction" that Harvard Business School Professor Max Bazerman holds the first day of each class. It is pretty simple. Professor Bazerman holds up a twenty and tells the class it will go to the highest bidder. There are only two rules in this auction. You can only increase by one-dollar increments, and while the winner gets the twenty, the person to come in second place has to honor the bid he or she made.

Bazerman said the bidding is always quick and competitive up until the twelve- to sixteen-dollar range. At that point people start to worry about the chance of losing some real money, so all but the top two bidders drop out. Bazerman explained, "The $16 bidder must either bid $18 or suffer a $16 loss." On and on this goes.

Bazerman said so far the record is $204.

At *Harvard* University.

In a *master's of business administration* program.[2]

The two Brafmans propose a number of reasons as to why this would happen so frequently among people who would seem to be able to make better decisions. Nobel Prize–winning economist Daniel Kahneman and Amos Tversky were the first to discover and chronicle one of the main reasons. They called it *loss aversion*: we are motivated not always by the more clearly appropriate decision (i.e., taking our sixteen-dollar lesson and getting out), but rather by a fear of losing. Once we get on a par-ticular path, we tend to stick with it. The longer we are on that path and the more we have invested, the harder it is to actually make a decision that runs counter to it.[3]

When you consider that more and more of us (including me) have lived the bulk of our lives apart from a meaningful rela-tionship with God, loss aversion starts to impact our search for God. I was freshly reminded of this as I spoke with a good friend of mine named Steve who had just decided to follow Christ. He was well on his way to receiving his PhD and was highly gifted in the areas of motivation and guiding people and movements of people. As we were talking, and as he was growing closer to making that decision to follow Christ, he said something very compelling: "I am realizing that the more I learn about Jesus, the more I need to unlearn the ways I have tended to inter-act with my world. I need to step away from some patterns and beliefs so that I can embrace ones that are more real and true." For my friend, who is highly professional, intelligent and in his forties, the stakes of that unlearning and relearning were high.

We are motivated not always by the more clearly appropriate decision . . . but rather by a fear of losing.

Our seeking of God, like my friend's, is subject to our fear of losing.

The $256 Teddy Bear

I am embarrassed to show how guilty of this I am. I had just started dating Tracy and wanted to impress her by winning a completely obnoxious huge white teddy bear at one of those carnivals that set up in parking lots for a few weeks and then move on. The game was simple; an old-school Coke bottle is placed on a plane sloping down and away from you. You have three attempts to use something that looks like a tuning fork to stand the bottle up. You can push only from your side and if it falls over, you can't stop it. You have three tries per play.

Seem hard to do? But the carny who ran the stand accomplished it with ease!

Your first play was one dollar. If you didn't get the bottle to stand up, you could play again for two dollars. The cool part was, if you got the bottle to stand on one of those three attempts, you got the bear and your three dollars back. But if you didn't, your next play was four dollars, then eight, and so on. Guess where this story is headed?

We made two horrified trips to the ATM in complete disbelief that we were in it that far. Ultimately we think we lost $256.

The guy ended up giving us the bear out of guilt. We gave it to some kid because it made us want to hurl whenever we looked at it.

John Clarke ran headlong into that same concept, but with much more on the line. As the structural engineer for the South Fork Dam, he could see what was happening. Even something as strong as a dam that rose seven stories in the air, and was as thick at the bottom as two-thirds of a football field, wouldn't hold under too much pressure. What happened May 28, 1889, was ultimately inevitable. His concern made sense.

The Brafman brothers would say the townspeople's responses made a lot of sense too. Remember, the repair had been finished eight years prior to the dam's failing. Eight years of business as usual makes it tough to argue the case that the business should be shut down. The hunt club brought money and jobs into the area. That was a lot to turn away from.

The reality is that we live our lives somewhere between situations as silly as pursuing a stupid $256 bear and being the lone voice warning of a danger no one believes possible. Between the inane and the impossibly difficult. And I think that we are a lot like those who built their houses at the base of the dam. When you live in the shadow of something that large, it is hard to doubt, and often, a few little leaks just aren't enough to make you feel differently. We live in a culture that reminds us often of how strong and powerful we are. We have so much control over our lives, and so much invested in our lives as we know them, that the idea of really following Jesus can seem just too big a change to make. Sometimes when I tell people that this very strong and yet very flawed world we live in cannot really support them, I wonder if I might even get the same looks Clarke got.

How We Make Decisions

There are some fair points for us to consider as we go through the process of figuring out just how safe we are in this world, the process of figuring out what we think about the job God has been doing, and the claims God makes. The first is that we don't typically come to decisions in an objective vacuum. Any number of factors determine the calls we make on issues around us. Living in a college town with a football team, I see this all the time. We are impacted by the opinions of those around us. When I need to understand the more subtle nuances of the Virginia Tech football program, I go to Mike Swann or Dave and Wendy Chinn. They are nearby and I have seen the amount of understanding they have. Likewise, people come to me when they are interested in some Bible-nerd piece of information or in how I keep my hair looking so rock-star good.

We all do it. Some level of categorization of people around us, as long as it is kept in check, is necessary. We need to know who can help us with what. Imagine if every time someone came to you and said something you had to assess his or her ability to be helpful to you in that area. Imagine not knowing whether the ShamWow guy was being straight with you! You would be forced to believe either everything or nothing, or research anything anyone told you. Neither is a good choice.

The problem is that we aren't always very good at keeping those categories in check. We can rely on them too much— something that should be a *part* of our decision process ends up being the whole process. We develop a sense of what we think about a particular person and that can often influence our decisions too much. We may miss the truth that is actually there, beneath the surface.

I distinctly remember the first few people who started to shake my belief that Christianity was nothing more than those elaborate Aesop's fairy tales we talked about earlier. At first, I couldn't even imagine that they were right. I had to sort through all my past and present experiences before I could give Jesus even a reasonably fair hearing. I had to work through the stereotypes I had developed and all the people I had seen who were not the type of person I wanted to become.

I had to sort through all my past and present experiences before I could give Jesus even a reasonably fair hearing.

That was when I realized I had really misunderstood Jesus. The process of sorting through my experiences and reality started seventeen years ago and has never stopped. To this day, I need to be able to look at him beyond everyday life difficulties, frustrations with the kids, or difficulties in the church I help oversee. Times where money is tight. Times when I peer a little deeper into my soul and realize that it doesn't look as much like the image of Jesus as I wish it did. Times like last fall when a very good (and much younger) friend of mine, a guy that I have copastored with for a number of years, was fearing a diagnosis of a pretty rare case of lymphoma. Or other times like what we experienced as a town on April 16, as a nation on September 11, 2001, or as a planet in the tsunami and earthquakes that struck Asia so violently.

I have to think through the issue of Jesus in parts, and I learned a long time ago that I need to slow down a bit to do that. Otherwise, life becomes such a confusing swirl that it can be tempting to listen to the most pleasant opinion I hear and just go on as if there really are no leaks in the dam. I either listen to anyone, or I don't think about it at all. Either way, Jesus, who is the God on whom my decision is centered, isn't really given a voice.

So, even now I have to regularly make sure I am getting back to who Jesus actually is—not who some louder voices might make him out to be, or who my experience in a painfully broken world threatens to make him be.

Even now I have to regularly make sure I am getting back to who Jesus actually is.

Another issue takes us right back to Mr. John Clarke, engineer. We all stand in his shoes in another way. The problem the young engineer faced was mostly hidden. Something was true of that dam, and he knew it. It wasn't a popular truth, and he knew that as well. But it didn't make the truth he knew less real.

You probably bought, borrowed, or received this book because you know how junky our world is. And that is a big reason why I wrote it. The brokenness of the world is precisely why we can look at God and wonder why he doesn't get in the game—why he doesn't step in, step up, or do something a bit more noticeable. We have had all we can bear of human trafficking and of governmental leaders' corruption that leads to the starvation of innocents. We hear and see people who die for the simple lack of clean water or mosquito netting.

We get that. So maybe if we were the ones living near the dam in 1889, we would have been the ones who sounded the alarm.

But I fear that I and many of my friends *are* seeing the leaks and the rivulets of water of this world we live in. Seeing the ways that our powerful position in this world is cracking, or already falls short—but then diverting our gaze before anything meaningful is really done. Perhaps we would rather see ourselves as John Clarke, calling attention to things that might seem unpleasant to those around us, but on closer inspection we might be more like those villagers who were trying to ignore a growing reality.

They weren't as safe as they thought.

Your task and mine is to assess who Jesus actually is and to make a clear decision about who we really are. My advice to you is to go to the Old and New Testaments of the Bible to find him. Seventeen years ago I began my pursuit of him. It has not been easy, but it has taken me on the adventure of a lifetime.

My Nondecision Was Almost My Worst Decision

When Tracy and I started dating, I was relationally stupid. Not "Aww, he's learning; it's kind of cute" slow. No, I mean clinically, relationally stupid. In all fairness, this was the first real relationship of great depth I had been in. I had been in some good ones prior, but this one was on a whole different level.

I had met Tracy while I was interning at a state psychiatric hospital. We worked the night shift together, she laughed at my jokes, and that was it.

As our relationship evolved, I had these minor relational panic attacks. If Tracy and I were around each other a lot, I would worry that she was suffocating me—even though I initiated many of our times together! And about once every three months I would hint at our breaking up. After all, I needed my space, right?

Looking back, I really didn't want to break up at all; I was just scared of the next step. So we got in this rhythm of the relationship coming under significant duress when I went through these times—until the last period of doubt I experienced.

Tracy got fed up and offered me a solution.

I remember standing in the kitchen of my rental relating my quarterly doubts, and she said she had had it. If I couldn't decide once and for all that I wanted to be with her, then she no longer wanted to be with me. I could tell it really tore her up to say that, but I could also see the resolve on her face.

She meant it; she was leaving me.

My lack of decision about her was really a decision about her. In my not clearly choosing her, I was actually refusing her. That was a new one for me.

My lack of decision about her was really a decision about her.

I guess in the back of my mind, my decision-making time extended indefinitely. I had all the time in the world, but Tracy felt differently.

God is telling us the same thing. Many questioning people don't seem to have any sense of a deadline in their decision-making processes. They are safe in their questioning and have little to worry about. But let me ask you a question: What if your lack of decision about God is more like my scenario with Tracy than you think? That your lack of a *yes* is actually a *no*?

I don't believe Tracy was trying to force me into anything that day as I stood in the kitchen. She was simply responding to my wishy-washiness.

Once again, we find ourselves in the shadow of the South Fork Dam. You and I don't know each other, but we have an awful lot in common. We are amazed at the world around us; we see its power clearly. We also see our own power, and that is pretty impressive in its own right. We have so much flexibility and control it is hard to see where that flexibility and control stop.

But if we are honest we would say we have seen other things, too, right? Like John Clarke, we have seen indicators that maybe we aren't as powerful as we might like to think. We have seen times we have gone the way that seemed best only to fail. We have seen people who look so wonderful on the outside be pretty terrible on the inside. Things we have honestly and genuinely trusted have shown themselves unworthy of that trust. These are the leaks, the indicators that something needs to be attended to. That the thing we trust so much might not be as trustworthy as we would like to think.

Those are times when the idea of a supernatural God who promises to be with us and strengthen us, love and accept us, can seem pretty good and tough at the same time. Yes, he will guide us in some directions we have not gone before *and* will show us that some pretty well-worn paths in our lives need to be avoided. But changing our path to join another story, even if it is so much better, isn't easily done. Like Tracy and me at the carnival, or the Harvard students, what we already have in the game matters to us. We haven't been standing still at all, have we? We have been setting up our lives and starting relationships and getting jobs and raising children and declaring majors; we have been *living.*

The idea of a supernatural God who promises to be with us and strengthen us, love and accept us, can seem pretty good and tough at the same time.

At some point, however, we have to acknowledge that the troubling signs of this world are pointing to a larger truth. We don't live in a safe place where all belief systems are equally good and right and fair, any more than we live in a world where everyone we meet is good and right and fair. Decisions must be made; those leaks have to be looked at carefully and their reality accepted. And we, at some point, must consider: is there anyone better to be loved by, coached by, led by, than Jesus of Nazareth?

Is there anyone better to be loved by, coached by, led by, than Jesus of Nazareth?

So, no, spiritual seeking and finding are not easy, and certainly there is risk. But what we get in return is far greater than anything we could give up. A world that is no longer subject to the whims of the faulty dams we have constructed, but one that is lived in community with the One who invented the rain. The realization that, while we won't be offered a pass on the suffering that our beautiful and broken planet levels at us all, we can be sure the God who originally created this world to be so much than it is now, is lovingly and fully connected to us and with us through it all. Even that we then get to become true agents of change to see this world brought closer to the ideal God had when he started it in the first place.

Questions for Reflection and Discussion

1. In spite of the South Fork Dam's size, when it was reconstructed a lot of shortsighted decisions were made that weakened it unnecessarily—some of those decisions were big and some seemed very small. Why did the people involved with the repair and building of the hunt club not see the dangerous position they were setting up?

2. If you had been in John Clarke's job when the dam was showing all those signs of weakness, how would you have handled it?

3. If you had lived in the area and if your livelihood was connected somehow to the hunt club, you had heard Clarke's concerns, and you had seen the leaks, what would you have done?

4. How does the Johnstown people's experience with ignoring signs of instability reflect our decision to trust a world that is showing just as many cracks and leaks as the dam? How also does it impact our desire to share what we believe is the solution?

5. Can you see how living for eight years with the South Fork Dam *not* breaking could lead those around it to conclude incorrectly that it *never* would break?

6. What evidence do you have from your life that would indicate what Bazerman stated, essentially that the far-

ther you go down a particular path, the harder it is to turn from it?

7. What implications does that have in a culture where fewer and fewer people are exposed meaningfully to Jesus in childhood?

8. What are ways we need to slow down our lives in order to give Jesus a fair hearing?

9. I almost made one of the worst decisions I could make by not making one at all (not deciding I was ready to commit to Tracy). Do you see any parallels with your own pursuit of God? Do you see how not making a decision to reconnect with God is very much a decision in itself?

12

Where I Find Myself

So, SHOULD GOD BE FIRED? In a word...no. I'm hoping you have already deduced that is the direction I've been heading. While this world is in much rougher shape than either we *or* God wants it to be, at least we can conclude that there are issues impacting God's decisions that we might not have been aware of. Perhaps you could add one more possibility to the list of questions that we started with: *As I look at the amount of suffering, pain, and outright evil in this world, I am left to conclude that either God isn't strong enough to stop it, doesn't care enough to step in, or simply doesn't exist.* I came to the conclusion that a fourth possibility was in order, and this is it: *As I look at the amount of suffering, pain, and outright evil in the world, I conclude that these are not evidences of a God who isn't here or is too weak or disconnected to care. Rather, I see a God who cares more about my suffering personally and the world's suffering corporately than I could ever imagine.* Yes, he does allow that evil to continue. Yes, he could stop it if he decided to, and one day he will. But as Peter said to his hearers back in the very first years of the church:

> God isn't late with his promise as some measure lateness. He is restraining himself on account of you, holding back the End because he doesn't want anyone lost. He's giving everyone space and time to change. But when the Day of God's Judgment does come, it will be unannounced, like a thief. The sky will collapse with a thunderous bang, everything disintegrating in a huge conflagration, earth and all its works exposed to the scrutiny of Judgment. (2 Peter 3:9–10 MSG)

No, we aren't limited to the three options of *not strong enough*, *not caring enough*, or *not real*. We have a fourth: he is waiting to give as many as possible a chance to switch stories, to turn to Christ and be adopted back into the family they were always meant to be in.

Blacksburg, Virginia, Today

I still get asked about the Virginia Tech shootings. Although it happens less now. Sometimes people even still recognize me from my interviews. That happens less now too.

But when I am asked about how things are going at Tech or at our church, I never quite know how the answers will come out. Most of the time I can answer such questions evenly—that terrible event is getting farther in the past. But still there are times when it just hits me again and tears come to the corners of my eyes, my voice gets shaky . . . you know the drill.

Sometimes strange things can trigger a sad response. It can be as incidental as seeing the number thirty-two (the number of victims), hearing songs that were played a lot in the weeks after the tragedy, looking at the newly installed door openers that cannot be chained shut, or even just looking at my kids and thinking about the loss that is still being felt by the victims' parents. There doesn't seem to be any rhyme or reason to what brings on the sadness. It just seems to come and go, and I try to be honest about however I happen to be feeling at that moment.

Things that would have likely gone completely unnoticed before now can grab me. What happened on April 16 is a part of me now, as it is a part of so many others. And I cannot imagine a point in my future where it won't be a part of who I am.

People typically ask me, "So when do you think everyone will be over it?" I never seem to have the answer for that particular question. Some people certainly will make peace with what happened more quickly than others. Some will find a way to move forward in much the same way they did on April 15. Some will struggle with the wounds all their lives.

I really don't know when or if it will ever be *over.* I just know that as God and I walk through my present with this in my past, I am learning a few things that I sincerely hope are working to make me a kinder and more loving person. A person who is, slowly, becoming more and more like Jesus.

**I am learning a few things that I sincerely hope are
working to make me a kinder and more loving person.**

Your Grieving Period Has Been Discontinued

A friend talked about the unique difficulty of feeling okay in
the aftermath of the shootings when everyone around him
didn't. My friend was asked some pretty direct questions about
his "emotional openness": Was he denying what he was feeling?
Was he being honest with others? He told me he didn't think he
was holding anything back. He said he even prayed that God
would make him cry in a public setting so that others would
think he was feeling the gravity the same way they were.

I have another friend who feels the same way for very different reasons. She feels as if people have some sort of timer in
the backs of their minds for how long she should feel sad after
something awful happens. She felt she'd been told, "Time's up,"
and she was still sad—this only made her feel worse.

Some well-intentioned friends have asked her if she is really
relying on God or if she might be allowing the drama of the
situation to carry her along. The formula that people seem to
use makes her healing so much more difficult. She would say it
looks something like this:

Proximity of Loss + Level of Emotionality − Months
Since the Event = Acceptable Amount of Grief

So, if you feel grief for too long, you're revealing some sort of flaw that proves you are immature or abnormal. I don't think I have ever been a slick or easy-answer guy. I don't lean toward answers to the really sticky questions in life that, when lined up in a teaching, form acronyms. And I recognize the complexity of our humanity enough to not give in to that kind of thinking. Tragedies of this magnitude in people's lives prove that life is messy. So interacting with God over the very real tragedies in people's lives will likely be messy too.

Interacting with God over the very real tragedies in people's lives will likely be messy.

My short answer for those who wonder when I personally will be over this is that I have absolutely no idea. I just know that sometimes it is easier to talk about and remember and other times it is harder, and I cannot seem to figure out which way it will go. Until then, I just have to be okay with going along for the ride.

I have experienced moments of great beauty, where it would seem as though I can see God's fingerprint on everything. But there are the other times when the anger and frustration come flooding back. And each reexperiencing of that grief and pain, whether personal or collective, has an impact on my faith. It has to. My faith in God—which, as I have said before, is really just my ability to meaningfully trust him—is an alive and breathing thing....At least it is intended to be.

Faith can grow stronger or it can atrophy. For those of us who are followers of Jesus of Nazareth, it is as real a part of us as anything else.

My faith in God is an alive and breathing thing.... At least it is intended to be.

"Well ya gotta have faith," as the song says. And this experience has caused me to look at my faith, not just in God but in others as well. I show faith all the time—so do you. I show faith in those on the road with me as I commute to work. I show faith in the people in line with me at the ATM, that they won't bull-rush me and take my cash once I have it. I trust that I won't get a spitter at a restaurant if I happen to send back an entrée. I trust that my daughter Emma will follow the rules of our home even when she is in someone else's, and I show faith in my hot wife that she won't leave my bald head and trade up. I show faith that God is aware of me and will honor what he has told me through the Scriptures. Certainly the level of trust we show is different based on the scenarios we are discussing, but our need for a certain level of ambient trust is not escapable.

That is the tricky part, isn't it? We have to have a certain base level of trust that the driver in the car coming toward us won't veer into us out of spite. But we see again and again how untrustworthy the people around us are. So typically we end up operating with the smallest amount of trust necessary and staying vigilant for when people will violate even that. In other words, we grow cynical.

Typically we end up operating with the smallest amount of trust necessary.

In the process, we can end up pushing not just others away, but God as well. We look at him as someone who has and will continue to let us down. Or we look at him from outside a personal relationship with Jesus and decide that is where we want to stay. Or we look at him and want in—we want God's acceptance and love that can be realized only as we come back to him through his Son, Jesus Christ.

Those of us who lean toward the cynical get there in different ways, but our challenge is the same: Drop the guard. Let people in more easily. We are called to do what Jesus of Nazareth did. He actually could read the motives and minds of people. And he was accurate. He saw their flaws; he saw how they would let him down when he needed them.

And he loved them anyway.

Now he challenges us to do the same.

A Brighter Future

Despite tragedies like the events of April 16, as I have grown closer to Christ over the years and matured in my relationship with him, love has appeared in my heart more and more. My heart turns toward others and not away. And my heart turns toward God and not away, even in the presence of the horror that this world can throw at me. Don't get me wrong—I still can have a quick cynical response, but over time, it gets weaker and weaker.

My heart turns toward God and not away, even in the presence of the horror that this world can throw at me.

I have also enjoyed realizing more and more that when I do hit the cynic button, I don't need to feel guilty. I have come to embrace more fully the concept of grace that Jesus spoke of and the Scriptures describe. I realize that I have been reconnected with God through my faith in Jesus, and I don't need to fear that God will take that reconnection away. God will not turn from me because I get cynical or because I doubt him or his goodness. In fact, God and I have had many very direct conversations together when I have expressed clearly my frustration with his plan or what I understood of it.

I cannot imagine those conversations will stop either.

I have always been a questioner and probably always will be. But without some sort of Pollyanna belief that only good things will come my way, I have come to a place of peace about God's reality in our world, his desire to be personally connected to every human on the planet, and even his goodness. I still go round and round about how his plan plays out: how much pain he allows and what he stops. Every one of the issues we have talked about in this book has been a big issue in my life with God.

Again, I cannot see that changing. But I cannot say that God should be fired because of my frustrations with him or the way he operates in the world.

I cannot say that God should be fired because of my frustrations with him or the way he operates in the world.

The main thing that has changed is the way I go through this world with God. In the past my cynicism would elicit doubt very easily. And once the doubt was started, everything else would stop. Now, while I don't automatically assume that my doubt is wrong (I never want to get to that point), I do have a process where I doubt my doubt.

The Doubt Button

My experience with God over the years has convinced me that he really is as deeply bothered about suffering as I am, even more. Increasingly, my anger at the situation has allowed me to turn to him. Becoming more mature in my relationship with Christ doesn't make everything great. But it has slowly replaced some of my cynicism with a real love and trust.

My maturity in Christ hasn't removed my doubt button—it has just shown me what to do with my doubt when it is released. Never heard of the doubt button? Let me tell you about it.

Everyone appears to have a doubt button. Some very trusting and loving souls have buttons that are quite small and tough to push. But others have buttons that are large and accessible. Whatever the size of the button, whatever the amount of force or number of attempts it takes to push it and start things moving, at some point we all have that button pushed. We doubt our spouse's motives, or our children's explanation of how the stain got on the carpet, or whether or not our bosses are really treating us fairly. We doubt God and his goodness.

Now, if the thing igniting our doubt is fairly small, we can let it go. But when that button is pushed too often or too hard, intimacy stops. We simply cannot grow close to someone we are constantly looking at out the corners of our eyes.

Consider this: What if your doubt button is too big? What if it is too sensitive? What if many of the times it has been pushed, it has been pushed in error?

Let's consider our doubt for a moment.

Doubt isn't bad. Doubt is simply a lack of certainty in something. It indicates to us that we need to get more information. You aren't godlier if you take everyone completely at his or her word without considering your past with that person. The Old Testament collection of Proverbs would call that foolishness: the same thing as seeing a danger in front of you in the street and walking straight at it anyway.

Doubt isn't bad.

In Acts 17 of the New Testament, one of the big-kahuna leaders of the early church, Paul, applauded the followers of Jesus from Berea because they didn't take his teachings as gospel, so to speak, just because he was Paul. He commended the Bereans because they compared Paul's words to the Scriptures to see if he was accurate. So doubt isn't an evil thing. It can actually be a useful tool.

Doubt vs. Blind Faith

A woman told me she just couldn't get to a place of blind faith. I asked why that mattered, and she told me that she couldn't follow any religion she didn't have complete faith in. But is that how it should work? It seems to me that my faith in someone or in God seems to grow in chunks. For me, faith and trust in God have grown in similar ways to my faith and trust in my wife.

When we first met and started dating, we had no idea where the relationship would go and almost no knowledge of each other. As we started to get to know each other better, I let her more into my heart and she let me further into hers. I began to trust her with more intimate parts of my soul and eventually grew to where I knew the next step in our relationship would be to ask her to marry me. Even after I kind of flubbed the process of proposing, she agreed.

About a year later we got married. But even then I didn't know her at all the way I do now. I now love and trust her more than I ever have. I needed time and experience to see she was worthy of my love and trust. Sure, she has let me down over the years, plenty of times; as I know I have let her down. Sometimes my disappointment was legit, and other times I was the one who was wrong, but our love and trust have continued to grow.

God uses the imagery of husband and wife to describe our relationship to him. In his letter to the church in Ephesus, Paul described the way husbands should be:

> Husbands, go all out in your love for your wives, exactly as Christ did for the church—a love marked by giving, not getting. Christ's love makes the church whole. His words evoke her beauty. Everything he does and says is designed to bring the best out of her, dressing her in dazzling white silk, radiant with holiness. And that is how husbands ought to love their wives. (Ephesians 5:25–28 MSG)

As I read this passage, I can start to see why. Just one of those ways of loving is a way that my trust will grow with Christ.

The woman who was frustrated that she can't get to the place of blind faith will likely never pursue any relationship with God, and she is in danger of missing the most important relationship of her life. But expecting to have that level of trust while you are still on the outside of relationship with Jesus would be a bit like expecting to read a bio of a potential spouse, read the thoughts of others who know that person, and deciding to marry him or her based on that!

The only way I have ever been able to progress in any of my key relationships is to give them a try and see where they go. Sure, good wisdom can help us all avoid unnecessary pain, but at some point, you realize that this thing won't go any farther until you go deeper. As much as I knew and loved Tracy then, I know and love her so much more now. And it has been the same way with God.

Doubt Your Doubt

If you had a friend who wanted to hurry into marriage with someone she'd met recently, you would wisely tell her to slow down, get to know him first. "Come on!" you'd shout. "Meet for lunch, grab some coffee!" In short, you would urge your friend to get close enough to tell whether he's worthy.

One way to gauge his character accurately is for her to pay attention to quiet doubts about his character. Use doubt as a tool to investigate who he really is. To see if a relationship with him could work, she would need to address her apprehensions. She would need to lower her "doubt wall" enough to get more information.

Use doubt as a tool to investigate who he really is.

In short, she would need to learn how to doubt her doubt.

As I have endured situations where I doubted God's love or power or concern, I have tried to approach him that way—lower my doubt wall to see if he is still as loving and powerful as I once thought. God is saying, "Trust me and let me show you the world through my eyes." He is willing to give us the time we need. But we need to lower our doubt wall to take advantage of his offer.

I remember a time when I had to rely on either God or myself. It was such a small thing, it probably doesn't even bear mentioning, but to me it was a big deal. I doubted that God would care, and I really didn't think he would move in that situation. When God came through, I learned to doubt the doubt that what I was going through really mattered to him. That doubt was good in that it caused me to look much deeper into God's availability and care.

Still, many times I have asked God for specific things that haven't worked out in my time frame. In a number of the cases, though, I now have had the benefit of watching enough years go by that I can start to see what God might have been up to in those situations. I have seen that in some of those cases, had he granted my request, the matter would have likely turned out worse for me than I thought at the time. Other times, as I am able to reflect back, I see that he *was* actually moving in those areas; it just took awhile for me to see it.

So I have learned to doubt my doubt. And sometimes I have found an acceptable answer to my doubt. Honestly that happens more than I would have predicted. Other times I don't get that nice quick answer. But usually, in those moments when I don't get what I would like, I still get something very valuable.

Over time I've developed a growing awareness that God is deeply in love with our planet and everything on it. He is saddened by what has happened to it, but he is very involved in its redemption and invites us to join him in that. If we are willing to try to trust him more, and are willing to not have all our questions answered in the manner we would prefer, we get back so much more.

Over time I've developed a growing awareness that God is deeply in love with our planet and everything on it.

Renovation: A Complex Process

Consequently, I have learned to be more patient. Some of the most important insights are the hardest won. I have learned that renovating my heart to look more like the heart of Christ is a bit like trying to renovate an old building.

In our last house the kitchen had a very unstable bar that stuck out from the wall. I remember the day I was scheduled to take the bar out. Very simple: take out the posts barely holding it up, cut the caulk line between it and the wall, take out the screw I saw going into the wall, and voilà! No more bar. After I did all that it still hadn't come loose, so I gave it a quick yank. It held. So, instead of pausing to reflect on the mysterious and invisible force that was keeping that bar connected to the wall, I decided it was time for some more force. So I gave it a strong yank and immediately learned how much damage a hidden lag bolt can do to drywall when it is torn out too quickly!

The same thing happened the day we were going to replace a light fixture. Simple enough: take the old one out and replace it with a new one. Right? I even went to one of those hardware store training workshops. I was ready to roll! But when we got the old one out, we found that all the downstairs electrical systems had been routed through that one fixture and not a single one was labeled! I spent the next several hours just trying to figure out what wires went where so I could label them and really see what I was doing.

During all of our renovation (as well as during our door replacement, window replacement, floor replacement, and bathroom fixture replacement), the only thing that went according to plan was changing out a toilet and even then just one of them. Had someone looked in, he or she might have wondered why the renovation wasn't happening more quickly. After all, it is a pretty straightforward process, right?

But an experienced contractor knows the truth. You never know what you are getting into until you start working on it. You never really know what is behind the wall until you pull the wall down.

You never really know what is behind the wall until you pull the wall down.

Our heart renovation is the same way. We think it should be easier than it is. But God knows our hearts too well. And he is a master craftsman who is willing to give us the time to walk through the process correctly. It takes a long time, a lifetime, actually, but it is so worth the journey.

So, yes, God has listened to my thoughts and emotions surrounding the shootings and other tragedies. He has heard your thoughts and felt your emotions about your public and private pains. And his promise is the same for you as it is for me. He doesn't give a timeline, and his process for taking us through it can be maddening. But the length of the process doesn't render his words untrue. I have never found the words of the Scriptures below (Ephesians 1:5; Matthew 7:7, my paraphrase) easily experienced. But I have also never found them to be untrue. Let them be my last words—for now:

If you ask to be adopted by me, I will do so.
And if you seek me—you will find me.

Questions for Reflection and Discussion

1. Has this book brought up any ideas you hadn't previously considered in your assessment of God's performance?

2. Have you ever fallen prey to being judged for your level of emotional response to tragedy, or have you judged someone else's response yourself?

3. Have you concluded through this chapter that there might be instances where you have your guard up too high too often? If so, how will you work to be more trusting with

and open to others (and in so doing, more closely reflect Christ), while still living in a world where everyone cannot be equally trusted?

4. Is there room in your view of God for you to be angry, frustrated, or confused by him and yet still believe he is handling his job well?

5. How big and easily accessed is your doubt button? What are some examples of when doubt helped you—and when it hurt you?

6. Once your doubt button is pushed, does all relational development stop? Are you willing to consider that we all at times need to doubt our doubt?

7. If you find yourself confident God is real and much more loving than you had thought, what are you going to do with that information? God didn't do everything he has done in order to be agreed with in theory by us. He did it to allow us to enter into a relationship with him. Ask him to adopt you—he will.

A Note from the Author

First, the more important stuff. I genuinely hope this book has been helpful in your spiritual walk. My prayer all the way through this amazing process has been and continues to be that God would in some way allow these words to provide comfort, challenge, or help in your process of pursuing him.

I know one book cannot answer a question as complex and emotionally loaded as *Should we fire God?* My own experience with God has been confusing, frustrating, wonderful, and illuminating. Questions about God's faithfulness and performance are ones I deal with almost every day, and I hope some of my thinking has been useful.

In case you're wondering how I injured my oft-mentioned shoulder, I did it when some buddies of mine and I had a contest to see who could jump the farthest through two hula hoops into a pile of beanbags. Yes, we were all completely sober. No, I didn't win. When grown men are seriously competing against one another by jumping through hula hoops . . . well, *winner* isn't the word that comes to mind.

Please feel free to contact me at jim@nlcf.net. I would love to hear from you!

Peace,

Jim

Notes

Chapter 2: You Never Forget Your First

1. Vittorio Gallese, Christian Keysers, and Giacomo Rizzolatti, "A Unifying View of the Basis of Social Cognition," *Trends in Cognitive Sciences*, vol. 8, no. 9.

Chapter 4: How Could He?

1. See cnn.com, especially "Red Cross Aid Rushed to Myanmar Victims"; and Pacific Disaster Center, pdc.org, May 2008.
2. See cnn.com, especially "Nearly 10,000 Reported Killed by China Quake," May 2008.
3. Glenn Puit, "Mother Sentenced to Life in Prison in Child Neglect Case," *Las Vegas Review-Journal*, October 6, 2005, http://www.reviewjournal.com/lvrj_home/2005/Oct-06-Thu-2005/news/3710996.html.
4. Ibid.
5. Richard Dawkins, *The God Delusion* (Boston, MA: Houghton Mifflin, 2006), 51.

Chapter 5: God Can *Really* Make It Difficult

1. C. S. Lewis, *A Grief Observed* (New York: Bantam, 1976), 4–5.
2. Dallas Willard, *The Divine Conspiracy* (New York: HarperOne, 1998), 86, 88.

Chapter 6: A Terrible Risk

1. N. T. Wright, *Surprised by Hope: Rethinking Heaven, the Resurrection, and*

the Mission of the Church (New York: HarperOne, 2008), 182; italics in original.

2. Joseph Lister, *On the Antiseptic Principle of the Practice of Surgery* (1867).

3. Ibid.

Chapter 7: God's Approach to Our Protection

1. Christian Smith and Melinda Lundquist Denton, *Soul Searching: The Religious and Spiritual Lives of American Teenagers* (New York: Oxford University Press, 2005).

2. John Foxe, *Foxe's Book of Martyrs*.

3. PBS, *Secrets of the Dead: The Great Fire of Rome*, pbs.org.

4. Ibid.

Chapter 8: Where Was God That Day?

1. *Westminster Dictionary of the Bible*.

2. Ibid.

3. Ibid.

4. *The Anchor Bible Dictionary*, 6 vols. (New York: Bantam, 1992).

5. C. Truman Davis, "A Physician Testifies About the Crucifixion," www.konnections.com/Kcundick/crucifix.html.

6. C. S. Lewis, *The World's Last Night: And Other Essays* (San Diego, CA: Harcourt, 2002), 86; italics in original.

Chapter 9: Okay, but Is He Good?

1. C. S. Lewis, *The Case for Christianity* (Nashville: Broadman & Holman, 2000).

2. C. S. Lewis, *The Lion, the Witch and the Wardrobe* (New York: HarperCollins, 1978), 86.

Chapter 10: A Look at Our Searching

1. Eugene H. Peterson, *Subversive Spirituality* (Grand Rapids, MI: Eerdmans, 1997), 35.

2. J. R. Woodward, "Is Conversion a Four-Letter Word?" jrwoodward.net.

3. Paul Ray and Sherry Anderson, *The Cultural Creatives: How 50 Million People are Changing the World* (New York: Harmony, 2000).

4. *Merriam-Webster's Collegiate Dictionary*, 11th ed., s.v. *cynic*.
5. See Diogenes Laertius and R. D. Hicks, *Diogenes Laertius: Lives of Eminent Philosophers*, vol. 2, Loeb Classical Library (Cambridge, MA: Harvard University Press, 1925).
6. Christian Smith and Melinda Lundquist Denton, *Soul Searching: The Religious and Spiritual Lives of American Teenagers* (New York: Oxford University Press, 2005).

Chapter 11: Praise Whatever, Whenever

1. Facts about the Johnstown Flood are taken from T. William Evans, *Though the Mountains May Fall: The Story of the Great Johnstown Flood of 1889* (Bloomington, IN: IUniverse, 2002); and David McCullough, *The Johnstown Flood* (Gloucester, MA: Peter Smith, 1987).
2. Ori and Rom Brafman, *Sway: The Irresistible Pull of Irrational Behavior* (New York: Broadway Business, 2008).
3. Ibid.

About the Author

Jim Pace has been on staff with New Life Christian Fellowship for thirteen years and one of their pastors for seven. In addition to the board of his church, he serves on the boards of the Network of Giving and Ecclesia, two groups committed to seeing our world renovated by the amazing love of Jesus. Jim is a sought-after speaker all over the U.S. on connecting the gospel and social justice, developing and enabling leaders for our culture, living a God-sized life, and many of the sticky issues of faith that confront us today.

Jim lives in Blacksburg with his wife of fourteen years, Tracy, and their three kids and dog, Elvis.